Catherine F. Johnson

Progressive Lessons in the Art and Practice of Needlework for Use in Schools

Catherine F. Johnson

Progressive Lessons in the Art and Practice of Needlework for Use in Schools

ISBN/EAN: 9783743389670

Manufactured in Europe, USA, Canada, Australia, Japa

Cover: Foto ©Paul-Georg Meister /pixelio.de

Manufactured and distributed by brebook publishing software
(www.brebook.com)

Catherine F. Johnson

Progressive Lessons in the Art and Practice of Needlework for Use in Schools

PROGRESSIVE LESSONS

IN THE

ART AND PRACTICE OF NEEDLEWORK

FOR USE IN SCHOOLS.

BY

CATHERINE F. JOHNSON.

———oo;o;oo———

BOSTON:
D. C. HEATH & CO., PUBLISHERS.
1893.

COPYRIGHT, 1893,
BY CATHERINE F. JOHNSON.

Norwood Press:
J. S. Cushing & Co. — Berwick & Smith.
Boston, Mass., U.S.A.

INTRODUCTORY NOTE.

It gives me much pleasure to say that I have seen the method of teaching the theory and practice of sewing, as set forth in this book, grow up in the public schools of Brookline, Mass., and can testify to the excellent results. The pupils have not only learned to sew well, but their study of drawing and English has been so combined with the instruction in sewing as to make it the foundation of an excellent mental training.

They also learn that sewing is not merely a useful handicraft, but an art, having its body of principles and rules, according to which it must be taught, to secure the best practical, as well as educational, results; that the fundamental principles of the art must determine the progressive series of lessons upon which the instruction must be based.

Any teacher who is an expert in the use of the needle, and will faithfully follow the method of this book, cannot fail to secure good results; and particularly, if she keep in mind that learning to sew is by no means the only end to be gained by the study of the subject.

I heartily commend this book to the attention of all who are in any way interested in the subject of Industrial Education.

JOHN D. RUNKLE,
Chairman of Industrial Committee of School Board.

Brookline, Mass., April 25, 1893.

PREFACE.

During several years' experience in teaching sewing, I felt the need of a text-book which would explain needlework from its rudiments and give directions for practical demonstration in class work. For my own use, I planned a course of instruction for the pupils of the W. H. Lincoln School, Brookline. Its use has given such satisfactory results that a demand has arisen for its publication.

For valuable assistance, sincere thanks are due to Miss Marion S. Deveraux, First Superintendent of the South End Industrial School, Roxbury, Mass.; Mrs. Joshua Crane, Member of the School Board, Brookline, Mass.; Miss Florence M. Starbuck, Teacher of Drawing, South End Industrial School, Roxbury, Mass.; and Mr. Arthur R. Wilmarth, Photographer, Jamaica Plain.

C. F. J.

Jamaica Plain, Mass., April 9, 1893.

CONTENTS.

	PAGE
INTRODUCTION	vii

CHAPTER I.

First Year's Sewing.

Class Drill. — Practice in position. — Practice with thimble. — Thimble exercise. — Holding the needle. — Threading the needle. — Making the knot. — Practice with scissors 1–4
Description of Sampler No. 1. — Materials. — Basting. — Stitching. — Backstitching. — Running. — Oversewing. — Hemming. — Buttonhole. — Crossstitch. — Buttonhole stitch. — Patching. — Darning 5–8
Questions and Answers 8–13

CHAPTER II.

Second Year's Sewing.

Work for this Year. — Measuring and cutting. — Paper folding and cutting. — Patching on paper. — Buttonhole. — Running and gathering. — Work bag . 14–22
Description of Sampler No. 2. — Materials. — Basting. — Stitching and backstitching. — Felling. — Running. — Hemming. — Oversewing. — French seam. — Name. — Felling. — Patching. — Oversewing. — Gusset. — Felling. — Tucking. — Overcasting. — Band. — Ruffle. 22–27
Questions and Answers 27–48

CONTENTS.

CHAPTER III.

Third Year's Sewing.

PAGE

Work for this Year. — Buttonhole making on flannel and on linen. — Cross-stitch. — Herringbone. — Feather-stitch. — Hemstitch. — Practice in cutting   49, 50
Description of Sampler No. 3. — Materials. — Hemming. — Oversewing. — Gusset. — Darning. — Hemmed-on patch. — Stitched-in patch. — French seam. — Oversewed patch. — Darn. — Buttonholes made with cotton and with twist. — Band. — Tucking. — Whipping. — Ruffling. — Marking initial and age. — Embroidered edge on flannel. — Flannel patch   50–55
Questions and Answers   57–68
Cottons and Needles used in Sampler Work 68, 69

CHAPTER IV.

Fourth Year's Sewing.

Work for this Year. — Patching. — Darned-on patch. — Darning. — Mexican work. — Cutting. — How to measure for drawers pattern. — Scale of measurements for different size drawers   70–81
Directions for Cutting Patterns for a Child   81–86

CHAPTER V.

Fifth Year's Sewing.

Work for this Year. — Measuring the form. — Pattern for front of tier. — Pattern for back of tier. — Sleeve. — Measuring for sleeve. — Front or upper part of sleeve. — Back or lower part of sleeve. — Basting and making sleeve. — Ornament   87–101

CHAPTER VI.

Sixth Year's Sewing.

Work for this Year. — Basting wide hems and facings. — To fit a basque lining. — To pin the lining to a form. — To form the darts. — To fit the under-arm pieces. — To fit the back. — To cut the back arm-size. — To fit the side form. — A plain round skirt. — To sew a skirt to the waist or band. — To cut a gored skirt. — Front. — Side gore. — Back . . .   102–114

# INTRODUCTION.

The system of instruction in needlework, as given in this book, is the result of many years' study of the subject, and of practical application of the methods in the public schools of Brookline, Massachusetts.

Experience has shown that careful preparation can make sewing as educational as any other subject of school instruction.

Drawings of the various stitches and kinds of work, with accurate written descriptions of the same copied into blank books for future reference; drawing diagrams of patterns from measurements; fitting the parts of these patterns together for garments; cutting and fitting simple dresses, first cutting to a model and fitting to a form which can be easily handled, afterwards fitting to a pupil's form, — all these can be taught step by step in a progressive course. Such a course tends, not only to train the hand, but to develop, strengthen, and mature the mind and judgment. By these methods, sewing can be taught in our schools with the most satisfactory results, and may lead both teacher and pupil to a clearer knowledge of the many beautiful possibilities of the needle.

When the kindergarten is fully established in the public school system, and its value is understood, the first sewing, that on coarse canvas, may be done in the two or three succeeding primary grades. But when there has been no kindergarten instruction let this work begin in the primary grade or the lowest grammar grade. The methods used in the class work of the first three years are given in the form of questions and answers at the end of each chapter.*

Questions for the day's work, not exceeding three in number, should be upon the blackboard, and if for any reason a child is waiting for direction in her sewing she can write the answers. When questions are given to a class, great care should be taken to frame each in a complete sentence and to have the child's written answer in another complete sentence, in which the point of the question is embodied. This creates a habit of thinking and of expressing clearly.

I. The position of the body while sewing is of great importance, because a careless attitude may cramp the arms and hands and also be prejudicial to the health. The chair should be of a height to permit the feet to rest flat upon the floor; the lower end of the spine should be firm against the back of the chair, the rest of the body free and erect, and the work never nearer the eyes than is necessary for a clear view of the stitches. The shoulders should be kept well back to allow the chest full expansion, and the head should not be allowed to droop so as to affect the circulation of blood to and from the brain. The arms should never rest upon the desk while sewing. The position of a pupil indicates the amount of interest felt in her work; if the attitude be free and alert, the mind will co-operate, and not otherwise.

While most children rest their eyes more than sufficiently by allowing them to wander from their work, there are, occasionally, pupils who need to be cautioned against fixing their eyes too intently upon it.

II. When a class is large, it is difficult to keep all the pupils at the same point in the progress of the work even in simultaneous instruction; the quicker ones are employed by various devices continuing active thought, such as assisting the slower ones or making a drawing of their own finished work on the blackboard and writing a description of this work and its use.

---

* A strict adherence to these questions and answers may not always be practicable; any ingenious teacher will be able to form rules and questions from her own idea of the needs of her pupils.

INTRODUCTION.

After correction, these drawings* and descriptions are copied into blank books for future reference. These books have been found invaluable.

III. The development of those senses which lead to quick and accurate perceptions of form and color is essential to artistic work in dressmaking and embroidery. This matter of taste is one of education, and should not be neglected. In the fifth year of sewing, possibly the fourth year, a pupil should be able to draw and color designs for garments, using crayons or water colors.

IV. From the beginning, a child should be taught to prepare her work in a thorough manner. Judgment is trained more in the preparation than in any other part of the work; on the sampler the short seams are easily prepared by the pupils, the colored threads and the varied work holding their interest and attention until more difficult work is undertaken in the second year of sewing. The most difficult part of preparation is first taught upon paper, the second year; this includes patches, bands, gussets, etc. It is helpful to use papers of two colors, — one to represent a garment, and the other showing distinctly the shape of the gusset.

Sampler work is adopted in the beginning, because progressive lessons in sewing can be more readily taught upon short seams. Afterwards these samplers can be used as reference for all future work, since all kinds of sewing are exemplified in them.

In the public school work economizing of material should be considered; the cost of these samplers is so small that they could be provided in the same way as all other supplies for the school.

The youngest pupils are given canvas in the first sampler, because judging of distances, size, slope, and direction of stitches are all made easier and given more exactness by the use of the coarse and even web. The second sampler is of unbleached cotton; the third, of bleached cotton.

---

* Several cuts in this book are made from drawings of the pupils of the W. H. Lincoln School, Brookline, Mass., and from the pupils of the South End Industrial School, Roxbury, Mass.

INTRODUCTION.

V. In the first-year practice in position, the use of the fingers and of the implements of sewing should precede actual work. Thoroughness in this is a safeguard against awkwardness and mistakes that otherwise would waste time and material. The class drill is given minutely in Chapter I. The drill secures prompt obedience, cultivates the faculty of observation, and trains the muscles for future work.

At the period allowed for the lesson one girl is selected to have charge of the box or boxes of cotton and of the needles. Whenever a pupil's work requires either cotton or needle different from that which she has, she makes known her wants and is supplied by the one having charge of the boxes. In this way every pupil soon becomes familiar with all variations of size, and understands what she needs and the reasons for it.

In the third year's sewing, a piece of flannel is marked 8, 9, 10, 11, 12, and one needle corresponding to each number is placed at the side of that number. This is kept in the work bag always ready for use. Small pieces of cloth for practice work should always be in the work bag, ready for a pupil to take up while waiting for the teacher's attention. When a piece of this practice work is especially well done, it may be fastened upon a sheet of card-board known as the "Class Card of Models." This may be considered an honor.

See description of work bag in second year.

Fig. 1.—Sewing desk.

VI. Each pupil should have a clean apron to wear in the class, or the work will soon become soiled; bags containing the apron, work, thimble, etc., may be collected and put away by some pupil after each lesson. This has a marked influence

INTRODUCTION.

in making children careful and neat. When special sewing desks (Fig. 1) are provided, the scissors stand in one corner of the waste pocket and the spools of thread with the pincushion and emery bag are left on the rod at the back or the side of the desk. Otherwise a teacher must use some device by which she can carry with her the things needed; a cord may be fastened on her apron, to which may be attached scissors, while spools, etc., are carried in the work apron pocket.

VII. If the day's work be clearly mapped out in the mind of the teacher before she goes into her class, and diligent use made of the two hours a week given to the sewing, most excellent results may be obtained by following such a system as the one given in this book. When a pupil has reached the fifth year of sewing, she has gained sufficient self-reliance to work with less help from the teacher.

VIII. The first sampler is composed of Penelope canvas* worked with colored yarns. In the construction of this sampler nearly all stitches used in plain sewing can be taught. The strips, when finished, are joined by oversewing to make the sampler.

The transition is naturally to a coarse, unbleached cotton sampler, and by the time a pupil has finished these two samplers, she is ready for finer work upon bleached cotton. Having satisfactorily made the three samplers, the pupil is now trained to the point of doing good work, and can proceed to the cutting and making of garments.

IX. When the uncut cloth or a prepared garment is brought from home, it causes endless complications and hinderances, and makes it impossible to systematize the work or teach the cutting. Therefore, it is considered more practical for schools to provide material used in the grade work, letting the pupil pay for each garment as it is made, thus lessening the cost.

---

* Coarse Penelope canvas No. 1 or 2.

GENERAL REMARKS.

1. Every child instinctively uses the teeth for biting the thread. She should be taught that she must never do this. It injures the teeth and soils the work. Never draw the thread under the little finger, but always over it. If the thread is grasped in the hand, it becomes dampened and soiled.
2. Never use a knot in sewing when it cannot be hidden completely.
3. Never let the scissors become too dull to cut well.
4. Never use a bent, rusty, or too large needle.
5. Never turn under a selvedge in a hem or a band.
6. Never hurry, especially in the preparation of work. However little is done, let that little be done thoroughly.
7. Never waste material of any kind.

THE ANNA S. C. BLAKE
MANUAL TRAINING SCHOOL
SANTA BARBARA, CAL.

PROGRESSIVE LESSONS

IN THE

ART AND PRACTICE OF NEEDLEWORK.

CHAPTER I.

First Year's Sewing.

In the first year must come the drill in position, as also a drill in using the fingers and all implements of sewing. Thoroughness in this and in all details of the work is important.

CLASS DRILL.

Practice in position:—

1. Instruct the pupils in the proper position, and the reasons for taking and keeping it.
2. Practice in distinguishing the right and left hands, also the different fingers.
3. Train a child to call that part of a thimble that rests on the back of the finger — the back of the thimble.

Practice in preparing the right hand for the use of the thimble:—

Raise the right hand, hold the thumb and first finger in a horizontal position, while the second or thimble finger is held vertically; then lay the first finger over the third and fourth, holding the three down to the palm with the thumb. This is a difficult exercise for untrained muscles, and the child should rest after four or five trials.

Practice with thimble: —

1. Give each child a thimble which fits snugly. Let her place it on her desk directly in front of her.

2. As in the exercise "preparing for use of thimble," raise the right hand in position; then, taking the thimble between the thumb and finger of the left hand, place it on the erect second finger of the right hand. Put thimble back on desk, rest, and repeat.

Thimble exercise: —

1. Again raise the right hand, and place the thimble as has been directed. Turn the arm till the palm is opposite to the chest; then bend the thimble-finger at the second joint until the thimble rests upon the top of the thumb. Raise the finger, and repeat the movement five times.

Fig. 2, A.

2. Raise the thimble just to clear the top of the thumb; and keeping all the joints limber, move the thimble-finger horizontally back and forth five times over the top of the thumb.

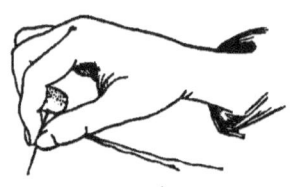

Fig. 2, B.

3. With the right hand raised and all the fingers free, bring the thimble-finger into the sewing position, having the front and back of the thimble parallel with the palm of the hand. Now make movements with the thimble-finger, as if the eye of a needle were resting against the back of the thimble. The thimble-finger is thus bent, and the needle pushed by the back of the thimble in order to exercise more force. . If this habit is once acquired, a stitch is taken with less effort than when the top of the thimble is used.*

---

* When a child has formed the habit of using the top. or side of her thimble, it is not always best to change, as a slow and poor result is produced, which is discouraging to her; however, in simultaneous teaching, all the pupils must follow the teacher's directions.

Holding the needle: —

1. Give each child one of the finest chenille needles, and have her place it on her desk, with its length parallel with the front edge of her desk, the eye of the needle to the right hand.

2. Let the child grasp the needle near the point between the thumb and forefinger of the left hand, and, lifting it, place it between the thumb and forefinger of the right hand, with the eye against the back of the thimble $\frac{1}{8}$ in. from the top. See Fig: 2, A and B.

Moving the needle as for sewing: —

Let the child move the thimble-finger as in the thimble exercise; and pushing the needle forward its full length, through a small piece of cloth or paper, slip the thumb and forefinger of the right hand forward and grasp the needle $\frac{1}{4}$ in. from the point, drawing it through the cloth. Repeat this movement.

Threading the needle: —

1. Give each child one of the finest chenille needles and a needleful of fine darning cotton.

2. Direct the child to hold the needle between the thumb and first finger of the left hand, with the eye uppermost and squarely in front of her so that she can see through it.

3. Let the child take the thread between the thumb and first finger of the right hand $\frac{1}{4}$ in. from the end, and pass this end through the eye of the needle, while, at the same time, she pushes the needle between the thumb and forefinger of the right hand, where it must be grasped, drawing the thread through with the left thumb and forefinger about 4 in.

Making the knot: —

Holding the threaded needle in the right hand, take the other end of the thread between the thumb and first finger of the left hand, and, keeping the thread tightly stretched, wind it around the top of the first finger and cross it over the end held between the finger and thumb; then roll the finger down the thumb, carrying the thread with it about ½ in., and with the nail of the second finger push the knot thus formed to the end of the thread.

Practice with scissors : —

Each child should be given a pair of scissors (5 to 5½ in. long), of the best steel and light weight. When using an ordinary school desk, have the scissors placed on top and in front of the child, the bows to the right hand.

1. Let the child lift the scissors by placing the thumb of the right hand through the bow of the broader blade, and the third finger of the right hand through the other bow, the scissors resting on the first and second fingers of the right hand for guidance and support. Let the child now push them from her towards the back of the desk, being careful to slip the blunt end, without raising it, along the top of the desk, and at the same time opening and shutting the scissors with the cutting motion as in use.

2. Let the child practise the cutting movement from right to left along her desk in the same manner.

3. Give each child a piece of ruled paper, and let her cut by the lines on the paper. Then practise cutting half-way between the lines and also across the lines.

4. Direct the child to cut two straight strips of stiff paper 4 in. × 2 in., and measure distances by holding the edges a certain space apart, according to direction.

5. Cut a 2½ in. paper square, using rule and pencil. Make this exact by placing the diagonally opposite corners on each other, measuring and paring. This is for a pattern for a canvas patch.

DESCRIPTION OF SAMPLER No. I.

MATERIALS REQUIRED.

4 strips of canvas,* 3 in. × 9 in.
1 strip of canvas, 4 in. × 9 in.
3 skeins of Saxony yarn, red, yellow, and blue.†
Chenille needle, No. 24.

For methods of work on first strip, refer to Nos. 12, 15, 16, in questions and answers of the first year's work.

For methods of work on second strip, refer to Nos. 20, 22, 27, in questions and answers of the first year's work.

Estimated cost of canvas sampler, 11 cents.

First strip of canvas, 3 in. × 9 in.

I.

Basting. — Make a line of basting ½ in. from the top, in red worsted, as described in answer to question 12.

Ten threads below this line make a second line of basting in yellow worsted.

Ten threads below make a third line of basting in blue worsted.

II.

Stitching. — Fourteen threads below make a line of stitching, using the three colors, each one-third the length of the line, as described in answer to question 15.

III.

Backstitching. — Fourteen threads below this make a line of backstitching, as described in answer to question 16. This is also done in three colors.

For joining the colors, refer to questions and answers 14 and 17.

---

* Commercial name, *Penelope* canvas.   † This will supply twenty pupils.

Second strip of canvas, 4 in. × 9 in.

IV.

Running. — $\frac{1}{2}$ in. from the top make a line of running stitches in red, as described in answer to question 19.

Ten threads below make a similar line in yellow.

Ten threads below make a similar line in blue.

V.

Oversewing. — Fourteen threads below crease the canvas for the whole length, so that the two threads will be on the edge; oversew this, as described in answer to question 20. Make the line in three colors, joining as described in answer to question 21. Lay the canvas flat again.

VI.

Hemming. — Eight threads below make one line of hemming stitches. On the lower edge of the canvas turn up four threads for the first turning of a hem; turn again, to make a hem of about $\frac{3}{4}$ in. Sew the hem in three colors, as described in answer to question 24. Join as described in answer to question 25.

Third strip of canvas, 3 in. × 9 in.

VII.

Buttonhole. — 1 in. from the upper edge and $4\frac{1}{2}$ in. from the left-hand edge, begin a buttonhole. Hold the canvas with the left hand, between the thumb and forefinger, working lengthwise. With a needleful of red worsted make three running stitches on the under side. Put the needle up from the under side, draw the thread through, cross diagonally four threads, take up two threads, with the needle pointing directly towards the chest; and proceed in this way until seventeen stitches are made. Turning the canvas round, make a line of stitches same as the first, with two threads between.

Twenty threads below, repeat this; fasten off the red worsted. Beginning with yellow worsted in the same place, cross each stitch until the closed end is reached, when the cross-bar must be made. This is done by making one stitch to the left, then one to the right, until three have been made on each side. Continue with cross-stitch until the starting-point is reached.

VIII.

Darning. — This is a series of running stitches in parallel lines, taking up two threads and going over two, beginning with one stitch in the first line, increasing to twelve stitches in a line, then decreasing to one.

Fourth strip of canvas, 3 in. × 9 in.

IX.

Cross-stitch. — Fourteen threads from the top make a line of cross-stitches, as shown in the illustration, three colors.

X.

Buttonhole stitch. — Twenty threads below draw the needle through the upper side. Take up vertically four threads. Then the thread from the eye of the needle is brought around the point of the needle from right to left, — care being taken that it passes over the other end of the thread, — and the needle pulled through, bringing the loop up straight to the top of the four threads, continuing these stitches across the canvas, in three colors.

Fifth strip of canvas, 3 in. × 9 in.

XI.

Patching. — Cut a small hole in the canvas 2½ in. from the end. Cut a piece of canvas 2½ in. square. Turn in the edges ¼ in. and baste on the under side of the canvas, the centre of the patch coming directly over the centre of the hole, being careful to have the threads match. Now cut the hole 1 in. square. On each corner cut diagonally across four threads. Turn in the edges all around, and baste to the patch.

XII.

Darning. — Let a torn place be represented by two lines making a right angle, as shown in the cut. Overcast these lines, taking up two threads. Make a line of basting all around, $\frac{1}{4}$ in. from these lines. In the corner of the darn make oblique lines of running stitches, being careful to leave a small loop at each turning, so that they will come together at the corner of the inside basting. The remainder of the darn is made by straight lines of running stitches back and forth, making small loops at each turning.

The first four strips of canvas, when finished, are joined by oversewing, the edges being turned down $\frac{1}{8}$ in. The fifth strip is joined to the others by a line of buttonhole stitches, worked over the raw edges. This finishes the canvas sampler (Fig. 3).

QUESTIONS AND ANSWERS.

1. On what finger should the thimble be worn? *Ans.* The thimble should be worn on the second finger of the right hand.
2. Of what use is the thimble? *Ans.* The thimble protects the finger, and helps in pushing the needle through the work.

   Show how the thimble should move in sewing.
3. How should the needle be held? *Ans.* The needle should be held between the thumb and first finger of the right hand, $\frac{1}{4}$ in. from the point, the eye of the needle resting against the thimble.
4. What part of the thimble should the needle rest against? *Ans.* The needle should rest against the back of the thimble, $\frac{1}{8}$ in. below the top.

FIRST YEAR'S SEWING.

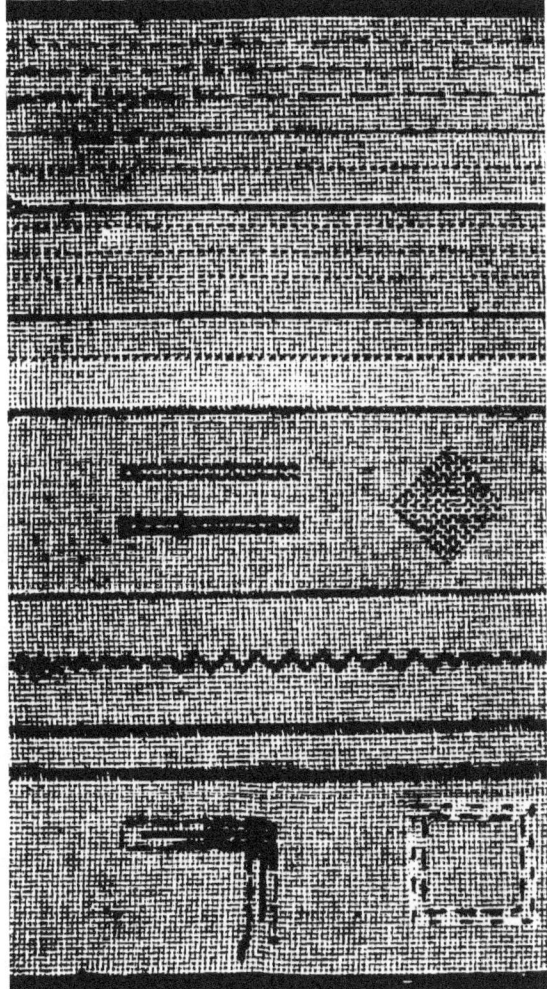

Fig. 3.—Sampler No. 1.

5. What is the back of the thimble? *Ans.* The back of the thimble is that part which covers the back of the finger.
6. Why is the needle pressed against the back of the thimble, and not against the top? *Ans.* Because more force can be used when both joints of the thimble finger are bent; when the top of the thimble is used, only one joint is bent. Stitches can be more rapidly and more evenly made when more force is used.
7. What is the name of the cloth on which practice stitches are made? *Ans.* The cloth on which practice stitches are made is called canvas.
8. What is the name of the thread used? *Ans.* The thread used is called worsted.
9. How is a worsted needle threaded? *Ans.* To thread a worsted needle, hold it between the thumb and forefinger of the right hand, the eye pointing towards the thumb and forefinger of the left hand, between which is held a loop of the worsted. Pass the eye of the needle through this loop, and draw the worsted tightly over it. Then pull out the needle, and push the loop of worsted through its eye. (Illustrate on the blackboard.)
10. How should the scissors be held? *Ans.* For cutting light cloths, especially woollens, the blunt side of the scissors should be underneath; then the point will not catch in the cloth. The thumb should run through the upper bow, and the third finger through the lower, the first and second fingers supporting and guiding the scissors. (Illustrate on the blackboard.)
11. How many kinds of basting stitches are made? *Ans.* Three kinds of basting stitches are made.
12. How are the basting stitches made on canvas? *Ans.* To make basting stitches on canvas, begin at the right-hand edge, the first line of basting $\frac{1}{2}$ in. from the upper right-hand corner. For the even stitches, pass the needle first under four threads, and then

over four threads, until a line is made across the canvas. In the second line of basting, pass the needle first under four threads, and then over eight, and so on across the canvas. In the third line of basting, pass the needle first under four threads, and then over sixteen, and repeat to the end of the canvas. (Illustrate on the blackboard.)

13. Is basting begun with a knot? *Ans.* Yes; knot the thread to begin basting, because the basting is finally pulled out.
14. How is the thread fastened for stitching and back-stitching? *Ans.* To fasten the thread for stitching and back-stitching, turn the upper right-hand corner of the canvas over the first finger of the left hand, and take up two threads on the under side with the needle, and draw through all of the thread except $\frac{1}{4}$ in., which is held down with the left-hand thumb, and take a stitch over it to prevent its loosening and drawing through. Then put the needle through to the upper side, four threads from the edge, and begin to work.
15. How is the stitching on canvas made? *Ans.* Begin to stitch on canvas with the needle four threads from the right-hand edge, on the upper side, and put it through to the under side, two threads nearer the edge, in a horizontal line; then take up four threads horizontally on the needle, and bring it to the upper side. This will be two threads in front of its first position. This is repeated along the whole seam. (Illustrate on the blackboard.)
16. How is back-stitching done? *Ans.* In back-stitching, take up six threads on the needle, then go back and take up the last two of these and four more in advance, and so on. (Illustrate on the blackboard.)
17. How is the thread joined in stitching and back-stitching? *Ans.* The thread in stitching and back-stitching is joined in the same way that it is fastened, beginning on the wrong side, over the second stitch from the last.

18. What is the difference between stitching and back-stitching? *Ans.* In stitching, the stitches touch; and in back-stitching there is a short space between the stitches.

    Show the difference between stitching and back-stitching by drawings on the blackboard.

19. How are running stitches made? *Ans.* Running stitches are made by taking up two threads of the canvas, then passing the needle over two threads, then taking up two more and passing over the next two, and so on.

20. How is the thread fastened and the stitch made in oversewing? *Ans.* To fasten the thread and make the stitch in oversewing, put the needle from behind through the two thicknesses of the canvas, two threads from the top and two threads from the right-hand edge. Then pull all but ½ in. of the thread through. That ½ in. of thread lay over the top of the seam, and sew over it by putting the needle up from behind and two threads in advance of its first position, then pulling the thread through until the stitch is tight. Repeat this over the length of the seam. (Illustrate on the blackboard.)

21. How is a new needleful joined in oversewing? *Ans.* Join the thread in oversewing the same as it is fastened in beginning, taking care to begin at the second stitch from the last one made, in order to make the seam firm, and sewing over these last stitches with both ends on top. (Illustrate on the blackboard.)

22. In oversewing are the stitches straight across the top? *Ans.* In oversewing, the stitches slant from right to left over the top of the seam.

23. How may the oversewed seam be finished? *Ans.* The oversewed seam may be strongly finished by sewing back over the last four or five stitches. (Illustrate this on the blackboard.)

24. How should the thread be fastened to begin to hem, and how should

the stitches be made? *Ans.* To fasten the thread to begin hemming, start two threads from the right-hand edge of the canvas and take up the two threads of the folded edge diagonally to the right and directly above; pull the thread of red worsted through all but $\frac{1}{2}$ in. at the end; put this remaining $\frac{1}{2}$ in. of thread up under the fold to the left, and hold it there with the thumb of the left hand; now bring the needle down and put it through the canvas below the fold, two threads in advance of the point at which it came out before, and pointing it to the left; take up two threads diagonally forward and upward. This is repeated for each stitch. (Illustrate on the blackboard.)

25. How is the thread joined in hemming? *Ans.* To join the thread in hemming, leave $\frac{1}{2}$ in. of the old needleful, and pull this down under the fold of the hem, the edge of which is lifted to place the thread under. Then put the newly threaded needle back and under the hem, as far as the second stitch from the last, and, beginning there, hem over these last three stitches and on to the end of the seam.

26. Should hemming stitches be slanting or straight? *Ans.* Hemming stitches should be slanting on both upper and under sides.

27. How should a hem be finished? *Ans.* By taking two hemming stitches over the last stitch; then run the needle under the hem back four stitches, draw the thread tight, and cut close.

Show these steps on the blackboard.

28. In what direction is the work done in basting, overcasting, running, stitching, back-stitching and hemming? *Ans.* In basting, oversewing, running, stitching, back-stitching and hemming, the work is done from right to left.

CHAPTER II.

Second Year's Sewing.

THE second year sampler is made of coarse unbleached cotton for the following reasons: —

The threads are large and easily seen without straining the eyes.

It is softer than bleached cloth of the same quality and more easily handled in preparing seams.

It is not so quickly soiled.

The pupil in learning to thread the needle for work on cotton cloth must use a coarse needle and thread, which should be used only on coarse cloth. Fine cloth requires a fine needle and thread.

Colored sewing cottons are used, because a child can more readily see her stitches and their shape, size, and method of joining.

The teacher of this class should interest her pupils, and awaken a desire to know all about steel, from which needles, scissors, and emery are made. Also have talks on the nature and growth of cotton, or tree wool, and its various uses.* Show cotton seed and tell the processes of growth until the raw cotton appears. Tell how the cotton is gathered and made into threads; how the threads are woven to make cloth.

Cloth has two kinds of threads; these are called length and width threads, or warp and woof. The length threads are always stronger

---

* "Every Day Occupations," by H. Warren Clifford, S.D., will be found useful as a reference, when studying about these raw materials.

than the width threads, because they must be stretched on the loom while the width threads are woven into them. When a piece of cloth is woven or finished, the length is readily known by the selvedge, or

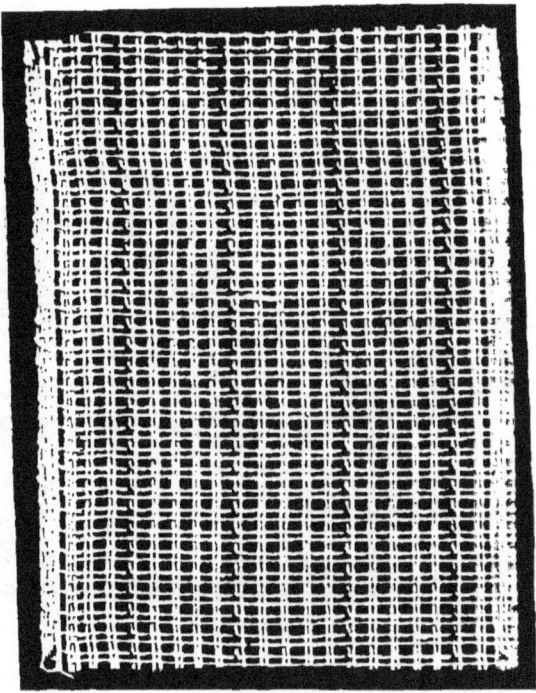

Fig. 4.—Canvas showing finished edges.

finished edge. The width is between the selvedges. The bias is the diagonal fold formed by placing the selvedge and width edge evenly together. Take one yard of the coarsest Penelope canvas (Figs. 4 and 5); hold this in sight of the class, and have the pupils tell the length and width threads, and how the bias is formed.

The pupil should make a drawing on the blackboard of a piece of cloth, showing the selvedge, cut edge, and bias; she should also express in writing the idea formed in her mind by these terms. A clear perception of all this, when once gained, will be a help in every lesson.

Measuring and cutting:—

The class should be provided with rulers, from which to learn the inch and its divisions. Have each child cut from stiff and unruled paper a piece exactly 6 in. long and 1 in. wide, to use for measuring; have the edges even and the corners square. This measure is kept in the work bag. Mark, as on a ruler, the whole, half, quarter, and eighth inches. The pupil must remember these lengths, as they are often spoken of in her work and in places which cannot be easily measured. Let the pupils space the different measures on paper and on the blackboard by means of dots and lines, using the ruler as a test of exactness only.

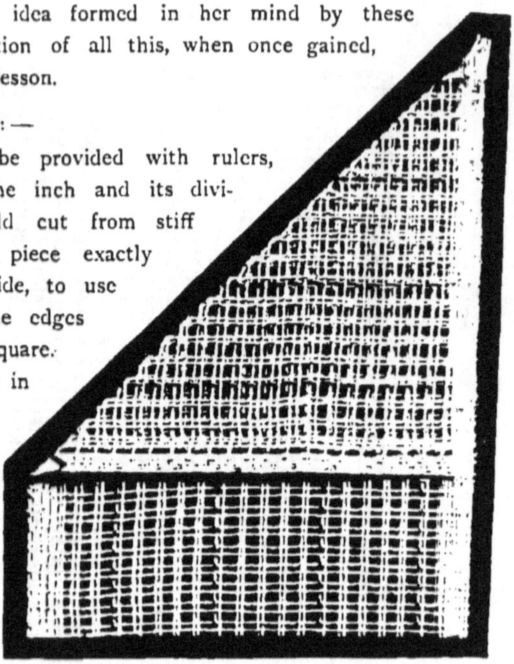

Fig. 5.—Canvas showing width and bias, or diagonal fold.

Folding and cutting:— I.

Give the child a piece of paper 3 in. × 9 in. Let her fold the lower left-hand corner over to the upper edge, and crease the diagonal

SECOND YEAR'S SEWING. 17

or bias line thus formed. Then crease the line parallel with the outer edge, to mark a piece 3 in. square. Measuring with this square, fold and crease the whole nine inches of length into squares. Cut the squares apart, and lay aside for patching in paper (Fig. 6).

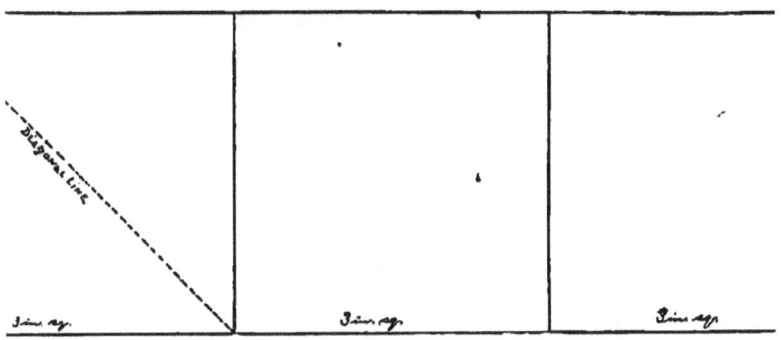

Fig. 6.— Measuring and paper folding.

II.

To represent patching on paper:—

Give to each pupil a piece of thin manilla paper large enough to cut from it a strip 4 in. × 8 in., to represent the size of the paper or cloth to which the patch is applied. Fold this strip into two 4 in. squares; fold again and again, making 2 in. squares. Now there are eight 2 in. squares. In the centre of one of the 4 in. squares cut an irregular hole to represent a worn place (Fig. 7). Cut another strip of paper 3 in. × 9 in. Fold and cut this into 3 in. squares for patches. Crease these patches into four equal parts (Fig. 8). Mark with a pencil on paper, or with a pin on cloth, the length or selvedge way of material and of patch. Turn a fold of ⅛ in. on the patch, then place the centre of the patch directly over the centre of the worn place, making the creases on material and patch match perfectly, continuing the preparation for sewing as described in answer to question 45. On the second 4 in. square make a stitched-in patch as described in answer to question 49. When this has been done satisfactorily in plain paper, give the class paper marked with even and uneven stripes. A striped paper of German manufacture has been found very good for this purpose. Several kinds of patches can be first taught upon paper.

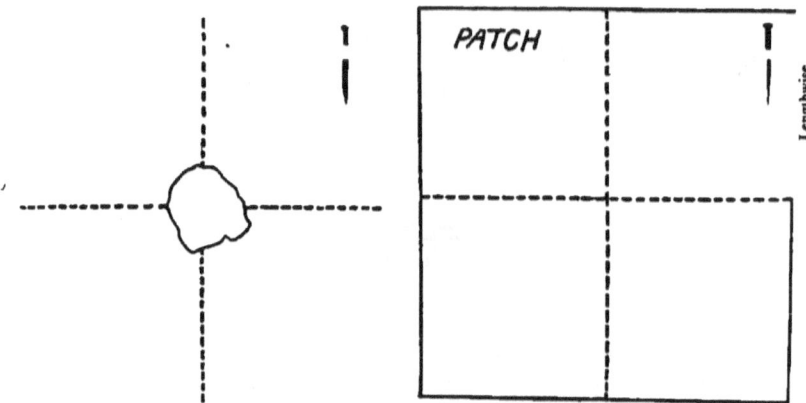

Fig. 7.—Paper folded on dotted lines for patching.   Fig. 8.

After patching on paper has been taught, the blackboard can be profitably used. Younger pupils are interested in watching the teacher as she makes drawings to represent a tier or an apron having a worn place, and a patch to mend it. Dotted lines across the worn place and the patch show folds which are to be applied to one another.

Now, giving a ruler and pencil to every pupil, let her draw and cut from striped paper a 3 in. patch; turn down ⅛ in. on the four sides. Then give to each pupil a small pattern of a tier cut in striped paper, with a worn place cut upon it. Baste the patch on the right side of the tier, making the striped lines on the tier and the striped lines on the patch match perfectly, the centre of the patch being exactly over the centre of the worn place. Baste ⅛ in. from the edges of the patch.

A patch well matched is less conspicuous hemmed to the outside of most garments; on white and many other kinds of cloth, it is better to sew the patch to the wrong or under side, as described in answer to question 45.

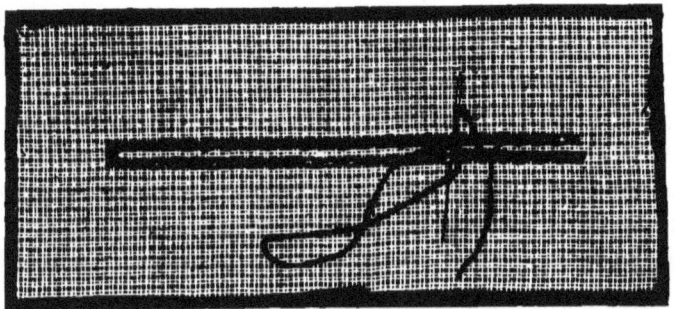

Fig. 9. — Buttonhole overcast twice with worsted (buttonhole stitch commenced).

III.

Buttonhole : —

Although the buttonhole is a very difficult part of the work for young children, if the method of making it is early learned it is a great help to careful sewing, and can be practised on canvas in the early part of the second year.

A fine needle and thread should be used in overcasting a buttonhole on cloth, because the edges may be overcast twice with a fine thread, and these stitches will not show under the buttonhole stitch when it is made with the coarser thread.

A buttonhole should be made with one needleful of thread, if possible. In case of accidental breaking, it can be joined underneath by a running stitch, while the unthreaded end is firmly held with the work by the thumb and forefinger of the left hand, and the needle put through the upper side in the loop of the last stitch, making the joining perfect. Diagrams of this work should be drawn upon the blackboard.

Explain the use of the buttonhole scissors,* and show how to find the length needed for the buttonhole by measuring across the button; then give the class a piece of ruled paper 3 in. × 5 in., and let them fold or double this paper across the lines; on one of these lines make a dot ¼ in. from the folded edge. Now, with the pointed end of the scissors, let the pupil make a small hole at the dot, and cut a perfectly straight slit the length desired for the buttonhole, using the ruled line as a guide. In order to acquire skill for well-finished work, the teacher should impress on the pupils the necessity of grasping the work *firmly* between the thumb and forefinger of the left hand, especially when working the buttonhole, having the thumb-nail just below the point where the needle is to be inserted.

IV.

Running or gathering:—

When a longer piece of cloth is to be sewed to a shorter piece of cloth to give additional fulness, gathers are used, as in frills and flounces; skirts are gathered into waistbands; sleeves are gathered into wristbands, etc. Test the firmness of the cotton before beginning to gather.

Gathering should not be undertaken until the running stitch can be well done. A piece to be gathered should be taken from the width of the cloth, as the fulness is easier to arrange, and the stroking has more effect upon the width than the length. A binding should be taken lengthwise of the cloth, because it will not stretch. These points must be carefully explained to the class.

The next step is the careful marking of the half and quarter measure of the ruffle and the band with a cross-stitch. The gathering thread should be coarser than the thread of the cloth. The thread should be

---

* Buttonhole scissors are not found in every home; and for that reason, it would be better to use ordinary scissors in this lesson.

a little longer than the piece to be gathered, and the needle large enough to carry the thread easily.

The thread is fastened firmly about a pin at the end before stroking is begun (see question and answer 64), as that part of the work cannot be well done if the thread is loose. A large needle or pin should be used for stroking, as a fine one would tear the cloth, which may be done also by too hard stroking. Any scratching sound is the sign that the stroking is too hard.

WORK BAG (Fig. 10).

To hold this and the following year's work, a bag is made of printed calico with a pocket on one side for the thimble, etc. One width of calico 24 in. wide and 28 in. long will make two bags 14 in. long and 12 in. wide and without a pocket.

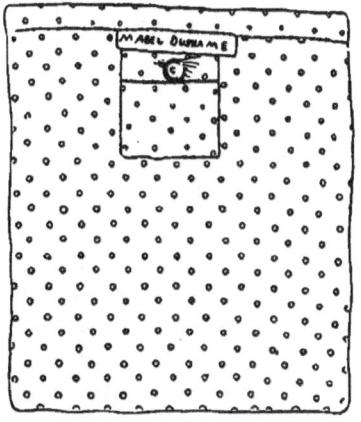

Fig. 10.—Work bag.

Making the bag:—

Tear the cloth lengthwise into halves. Double one strip of cloth in the centre and oversew the selvedges. Stitch the raw edges together and overcast. Make a hem ¾ in. wide at the top. The pocket can be made of a small piece of calico 3 in. wide and 4 in. long with a hem 1 in. wide. When a pupil has learned to make a buttonhole, let her make one in the middle of this hem, lengthwise with the pocket; turn in ¼ in. of the three raw edges; now the pocket is 3 in. long and 2½ in. wide, and is hemmed to the bag, the hem of the bag being a guide to the placing of the pocket. The thimble, small spool of silk, etc., can be carefully kept in this pocket.

A small piece of tape 1 in. square is sewed on the inside of the bag, as a stay for the button. The button is sewed on the bag, opposite to the buttonhole in the pocket. Now the pupil first prints with a pencil and then stitches her name on a piece of tape, which is sewed directly over the pocket.

Work bags should never be drawn with strings, as that will crush the work and make it look untidy. After the work is neatly placed inside, and a pupil selected to collect them, the bags should be placed in a box or drawer until the next lesson.

If this care is taken, the work can be more quickly distributed, and pupils may begin to work in a very short time after being seated. To allow children, who are working at the same point on their samplers, to sit near each other, has been found to excite the ambition of all.

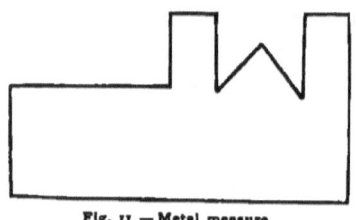

Fig. 11.—Metal measure.

A pupil should always have in her bag pieces of white cotton, silesia, and woollen cloths, in which one, two, three, or more buttonholes have been cut. Whenever there come moments of waiting for the teacher, or at other unoccupied times, the pupil should practise buttonhole making on these, according to the rules which have been given; a perfectly made buttonhole being given her as a model.

A metal measure of the shape here shown (Fig. 11) will be found very useful. It combines measurements of the various tucks and hems used in samplers.

DESCRIPTION OF SAMPLER No. 2.

MATERIALS REQUIRED.

Eight strips of unbleached cotton cloth (seven torn lengthwise, one torn from the width for a ruffle) 9 in. × 3 in. Two pieces of the same 3 in. square, for patches. $1\frac{1}{2}$ in. square of the same, for a gusset.

One strip of striped or checked cloth 9 in. × 3 in. with selvedge on one side. Two pieces of the same 3 in. square, for patches. Red, yellow, and blue spool cotton, No. 40. Needles No. 8. One porcelain button. Estimated cost of unbleached sampler, 15 cts.

DIRECTIONS FOR MAKING THE SAMPLER.

I.

Basting. — Baste two strips together $\frac{1}{2}$ in. from the top edge with red cotton, the stitches $\frac{1}{4}$ in. long and the spaces between $\frac{1}{4}$ in. long.

$\frac{1}{2}$ in. below, a second line of basting in yellow.

$\frac{1}{2}$ in. below, a third line of basting in blue.

$\frac{1}{2}$ in. below, a fourth line of basting, like the second line. Make these basting stitches of different lengths, as on canvas samplers.

II.

Stitching and back-stitching. — Stitch with yellow and blue cotton close below the first basting, and with yellow and red below the fourth basting.

III.

Hem felling. — Cut off the under piece of cloth $\frac{1}{4}$ in. below the line of back-stitching, turn the edge under $\frac{1}{2}$ in. at a time with needle, and hem with three colors.

IV.

Running. — Three rows of running stitches below this, one of each color, red, yellow, and blue. Keep the needle in the cloth all the time, as in basting.

V.

Hemming. — Take a third strip of cloth, turn one edge down $\frac{1}{8}$ in. and turn again with a metal measure $\frac{3}{4}$ in. ; baste edge of hem, then hem with three colors.

VI.

Oversewing. — Turn down the edge of the first strip $\frac{1}{8}$ in. and baste to edge of hem; then oversew with three colors.

VII.

French seam. — Put a fourth strip to the wrong side of the third and baste on the right side, $\frac{1}{4}$ in. from the top; make a line of two running stitches and a back-stitch just below the basting; cut off the edges $\frac{1}{8}$ in. above the sewing and turn the seam the other side out; crease hard, stitch with three colors just below the raw edges of the first seam, so as to close them.

VIII.

Name. — Print the pupil's name with a pencil in the middle of this strip, and stitch with any color preferred directly on the pencil marks.

IX.

Felling. — Baste the raw edge of the fifth strip to the fourth $\frac{1}{4}$ in. below the top edge and stitch with the three colors; then cut the edge of the under side $\frac{1}{8}$ in. above the line of stitching, and the edge of upper side $\frac{1}{4}$ in. above stitching. Open the seam flat, turn the broader edge under with the needle, and hem with three colors, making a fell.

X.

Patching. — Cut two small holes 3 in. from either end of the last strip and midway between the fell and the selvedge. Mend one hole with hemmed-on patch (question and answer 45), and the other with stitched-in patch (question and answer 49).

XI.

Patching. — Take a piece of striped or checked cloth for the sixth strip, cut holes as in the fifth strip, and make a stitched-in patch and an

SECOND YEAR'S SEWING.

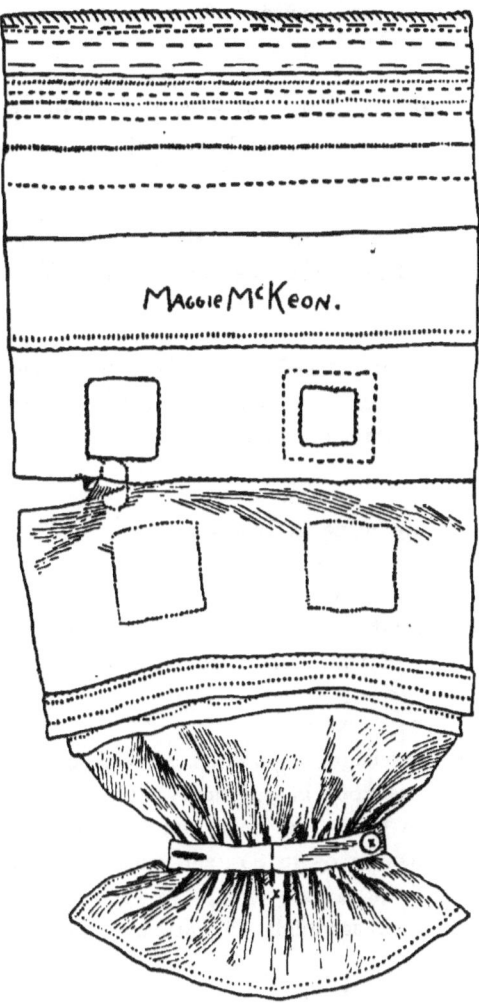

Fig. 12.—Sampler No. 2.

oversewed patch (question and answer 50), matching the stripes or checks.

XII.

Oversewing. — Turn down one edge $\frac{1}{8}$ in. and baste to the selvedge of the last strip, then oversew with two colors, leaving $2\frac{1}{2}$ in. unsewed.

XIII.

Gusset. — A gusset is put into the opening between the unbleached cotton and the striped or checked cloth, according to question and answer 53.

XIV.

Felling. — The sixth strip of unbleached cotton is then basted to the striped cloth and a fell made, using running and back stitch, instead of stitching, for the first seam of the fell.

XV.

Tucking. — Two $\frac{1}{4}$ in. tucks are made in this strip according to question and answer 55.

XVI.

Overcasting seams. — The seventh strip is joined by a running and back stitched seam, the edges of which are evenly cut and overcast with three colors.

XVII.

Putting on a band. — The other edge is gathered, stroked, and put into a band 2 in. × $4\frac{1}{2}$ in., as described in questions and answers 61 to 66.

A buttonhole is then cut in the band and overcast with No. 70 cotton (questions and answers 67 to 80), and worked with any color desired, 40 cotton (questions and answers 71 to 73).

A button is sewed on according to questions and answers 74 to 75.

XVIII.

Hemmed and whipped ruffle. — Make a $\frac{1}{8}$ in. hem on one edge and on the sides of the eighth strip. Mark the centre with a cross-stitch with the blue cotton. Mark the centre of the band in the same way. Whip the raw edge of the ruffle and oversew to the band (question and answer 76 and 77). (Fig. 12.)

QUESTIONS AND ANSWERS.

1. Cloth. What kind of cloth is now used? *Ans.* Unbleached cloth.
2. Why is this kind of cloth used? *Ans.* Because it is made without dressing and is easier to handle while learning to sew and to prepare the seams.
3. Is unbleached cloth the only kind made without dressing? *Ans.* No, bleached cotton and a great many kinds of cloth are made without dressing. (*Memorandum to Teacher.* Show a kind of fabric made with and without dressing.)
4. Then why is not undressed, bleached cotton now used? *Ans.* Because undressed, bleached cotton is made with finer threads and is not so easy to prepare seams upon; a fine needle must be used when using fine cloth.
5. What number needle and thread is used on this unbleached cloth? *Ans.* No. 8 needle and No. 40 thread is used.
6. What length of thread should be used? *Ans.* A thread 10 in. long should be used on the unbleached sampler. (*Memorandum to Teacher.* Make plain to the pupils how time is wasted by drawing a long thread through the cloth, how work can be better and more rapidly done with a short thread.)
7. How many different colored threads are used for this sampler? *Ans.* Three different colors are used. Red, blue, and yellow or orange.
8. Why are these different colors used? *Ans.* To make the stitches plain, and show how neatly thread can be joined.

9. How can twisted or kinked thread be avoided or remedied? *Ans.* Kinking can be avoided by not twisting the thread in sewing; if kinking does come, drop the threaded needle while fastened to the work, and the weight of the needle will unwind all extra twist. (Practice for position when sewing, etc. See exercise in first year.)
10. What is the first work upon this sampler? *Ans.* The first work is basting, with stitches of three different lengths.
11. How is a seam formed? *Ans.* A seam is formed by basting or sewing together two or more pieces of cloth.
12. What is the difference between sewing and basting a seam? *Ans.* Basting is slight sewing, with long or short stitches, while sewing is made with small firm stitches.
13. How is a seam basted for stitching or back-stitching? *Ans.* It is basted ¼ in. from the edge.
14. How long are basting stitches made for a stitched or back-stitched seam? *Ans.* For a stitched or back-stitched seam, make the basting stitches ¼ in. long and the space between ⅛ in.
15. In basting for seams should the thread be drawn through the cloth after taking each stitch? *Ans.* No; work with the needle in the cloth throughout its length (Fig. 13).

Fig. 13.—Basting.

16. How is this done? *Ans.* After making seven stitches, the cloth becomes crowded, and then the point of the needle in the cloth should be held between the thumb and first finger of the left hand, and the first four stitches taken should be pushed off the eye of the needle with the thumb and first finger of the right hand; then three more stitches should be made, and those nearest the eye pushed back in the same way, until the seam is

SECOND YEAR'S SEWING.

basted. Gathering is done in the same way, but with small stitches. (Illustrate on the blackboard.)

17. Why is it better to baste for a seam in this way? *Ans.* Because it saves much time, and makes a straighter guide by which to sew.*
18. Is a hem basted in this way? *Ans.* No, a hem has a straight edge which can be the guide, and the basting line is made $\frac{1}{8}$ in. from the lower edge of the hem with one or more stitches on the needle before the thread is drawn through the cloth, making the basting stitch $\frac{1}{4}$ in. long and the spaces between $\frac{1}{8}$ in. long.
19. How is basting done for oversewing? *Ans.* The bastings are made for oversewing $\frac{1}{8}$ in. below the top edge — the stitches $\frac{1}{4}$ in. long and spaces between $\frac{1}{8}$ in. long.
20. Why is basting for oversewing made near the edge? *Ans.* That the edges may be held together firmly.
21. When a seam is basted, where is the line of stitching made? *Ans.* The stitching is always below and as near the basting as possible.
22. Is a knot used in beginning to stitch? *Ans.* No; in beginning to stitch the thread is fastened on the under side by one stitch and a back-stitch.
23. What colors are used in stitching the first line? *Ans.* Yellow and blue are used.
24. What kind of sewing is made under the fourth line of basting? *Ans.* Back-stitching is made under the fourth line of basting.
25. What is the difference between stitching and back-stitching? *Ans.* In stitching the stitches touch, in back-stitching there is a small space between the stitches (Figs. 14 and 15).

---

* Fabrics that crush easily cannot be basted in this way.

26. What colors are here used? *Ans.* Yellow and red are used.
27. How is a stitched or back-stitched seam finished? *Ans.* A stitched or back-stitched seam is finished by sewing back over the last three stitches.
28. When should stitching and when back-stitching be used? *Ans.* When much wear or strain comes upon a seam, it should be stitched, otherwise it can be back-stitched.

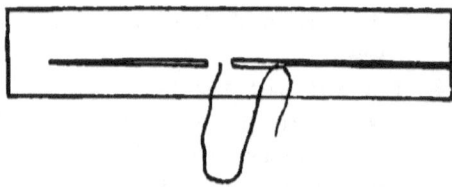

Fig. 14. — Stitching.*

29. How are running stitches made? *Ans.* The same way as basting, but with smaller stitches.
30. Why is the needle not drawn through the cloth at every few stitches in making running stitches? *Ans.* In running for gathering the needle is not drawn out until a certain part of the cloth is gathered or the needleful of thread is used, because the longer the needle is kept in the cloth, the straighter will be the seam and the quicker the work.

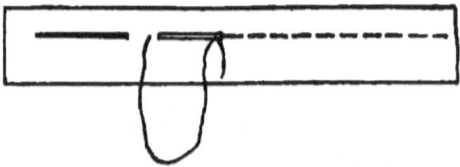

Fig. 15. — Back-stitching.*

But in running tucks, where the cloth is double, the needle is taken out every third or fourth stitch according to the thickness of the cloth.
31. How can a broad hem be kept straight? *Ans.* By using a measure of the right width and basting carefully.

---

* Stitching, or back-stitching, as it is sometimes called, is the work which the sewing machine imitates so accurately; two definitions are here given, because there are two different methods of working it, — one where strength is the important feature, and one where strength is not so important.

SECOND YEAR'S SEWING.

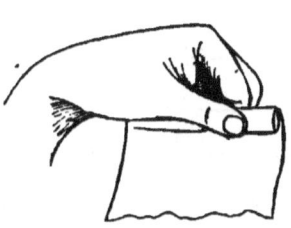

Fig. 16.—Hem turned.

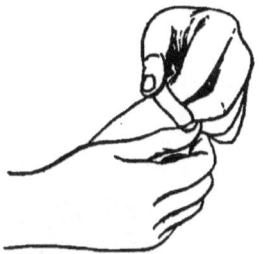

Fig. 17.—Placing work on the finger for hemming.

32. How should the hem be held for sewing? *Ans.* The edge of the hem to be sewed is placed over the first finger of the left hand

Fig. 18.—Held over the finger for hemming.

Fig. 19.—Needle pointing to the centre of left thumb-nail, when hemming.

$\frac{1}{2}$ in. from the end of the finger, held in place with the thumb and second finger (Figs. 16, 17, 18). Sew with the needle point-

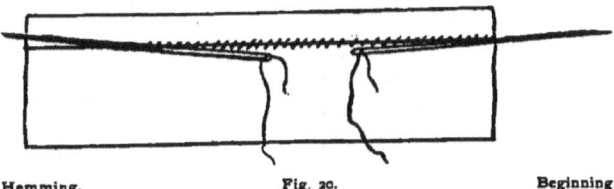

Hemming. Fig. 20. Beginning.

ing to the middle of the edge of the left thumb-nail (Fig. 19). Make the stitches small, but to show distinctly on the under side. (Illustrate on the blackboard.)

Fig. 21.—Work held for oversewing.

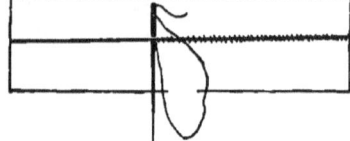

Fig. 22.—Oversewing.

33. How should the work be held for oversewing? *Ans.* The work should be held around the end of the first finger of the left hand, and kept firmly in place with the thumb and second finger (Fig. 21).
34. How should the needle be pointed in oversewing? *Ans.* In oversewing the needle should be pointed directly toward the chest (Fig. 22).
35. What must always be done after the seam is oversewed? *Ans.* Press the stitches flat on the wrong side, with the right thumb-nail, to finish the oversewing seam.
36. When is an oversewed seam used? *Ans.* An oversewed seam is used in joining two selvedges or two folded edges.
37. What is a selvedge? *Ans.* A woven or finished edge.
38. What is a raw edge? *Ans.* A cut or torn edge.
39. What is overcasting? *Ans.* Overcasting is the same as oversewing, the stitches being larger, and is used over raw edges to prevent them from ravelling (Fig. 23).

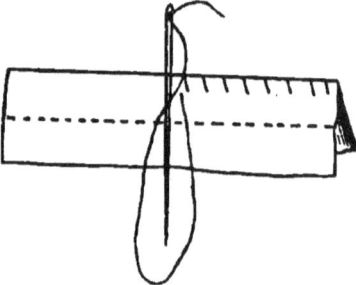

Fig. 23.—Overcasting.

40. How do we begin the work and join the thread in overcasting? *Ans.* We should tie a knot in the end of the thread, and put it between the two edges of the cloth, so that it cannot be seen.
41. When is a French seam used? *Ans.* A French seam is used on delicate material to conceal the raw edges.
42. In making a fell, how should the work be held in order to turn the edge with the needle? *Ans.* The work should be held as for hemming, but more firmly.
43. How should the needle be held in order to turn the edge of the fell? *Ans.* The needle should be held nearly parallel with the seam, the eye resting on the thimble, and grasped firmly near the centre by the thumb and forefinger of the right hand. Thus held, the edge of the fell should be turned under with the point of the needle ½ in.; when that is hemmed another ½ in. is turned, until the seam is finished (Fig. 24).

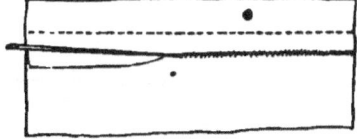

Fig. 24.

44. When is a fell used? *Ans.* A fell is used when a flat seam without raw edges is required.
45. How is a hemmed-on patch made? *Ans.* A square piece of cloth is turned down ⅛ in. on its four edges, selvedge sides first, and basted over the worn or torn place, on the under side, being careful that the length and width threads match the cloth, and then neatly hemmed down. The torn edges on the right side are then cut evenly to ¾ in. from the hemmed square, and a short bias cut made in each corner. The four edges are then turned under evenly and hemmed down on to the patch (Figs. 25, 26). Represent this on the blackboard in the different stages.
46. What is a bias cut? *Ans.* A bias cut is a cut made diagonally across the warp and the woof.

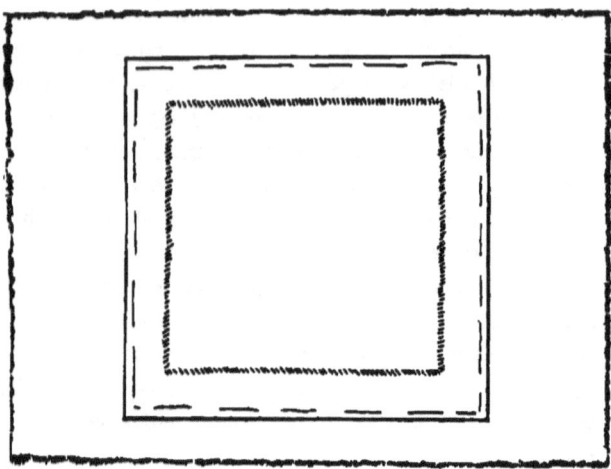

Fig. 25.—A hemmed-on patch. Under or wrong side.

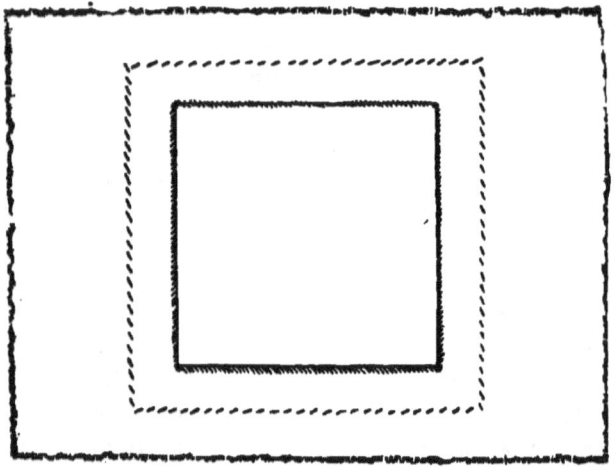

Fig. 26.—A hemmed-on patch. Upper or right side.

47. What is the warp? *Ans.* The threads that run up and down or lengthwise of the cloth are called the warp.
48. What is the woof? *Ans.* The threads that run across the cloth from one selvedge to the other are called the woof. (Show these on the blackboard.)
49. How is a stitched-in patch made? *Ans.* The worn or torn part is first cut out in a square (see Fig. 28). The straight edges of the hole are made true by a drawn thread; then two adjoining sides are folded evenly together, and a bias cut ¼ in. is made at each of the four corners, and the edges of the hole thus cut are folded and creased down on the under side ¼ in. (see dotted lines in Fig. 28). Then a square piece is basted to these creases, so that it lies perfectly smooth at the corners. Be sure to begin and end the basting on the *patch*, to make smooth and square corners (Figs. 27, 28, 29, 30, 31). Represent this on the blackboard in the different stages.

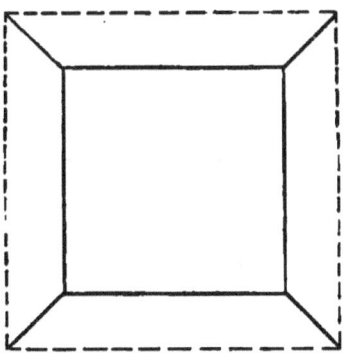

Fig. 28. — Worn place cut out; the cloth prepared for a stitched-in patch.

50. How is an oversewed patch made? *Ans.* The torn part is cut out and prepared in the same way as for a stitched-in patch; then the square piece of cloth to be set in is turned down by a thread evenly on one side, and oversewed, on the under side, to one side of the prepared hole from corner to corner. The second, third, and fourth sides are oversewed in the same way. Great care must be taken to turn the edges evenly, so that the patch may be flat when finished (Figs. 32, 33). (Show this on the blackboard.)
51. What is a gusset? *Ans.* A gusset is a piece of cloth used to strengthen the ends of a seam.

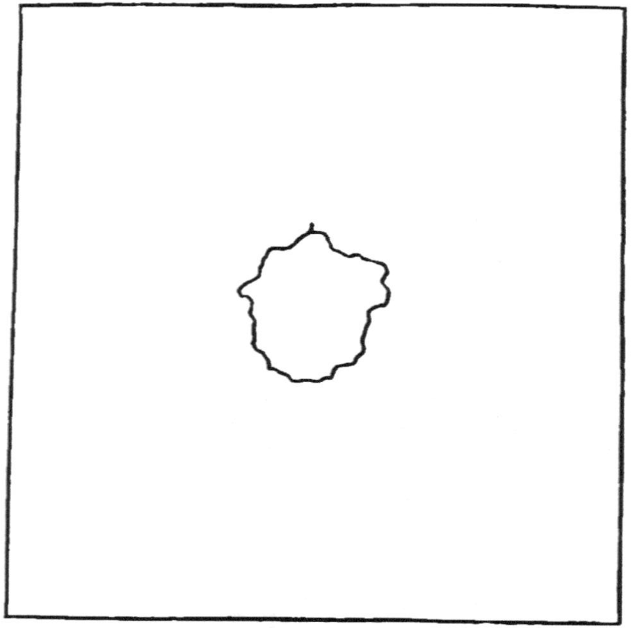

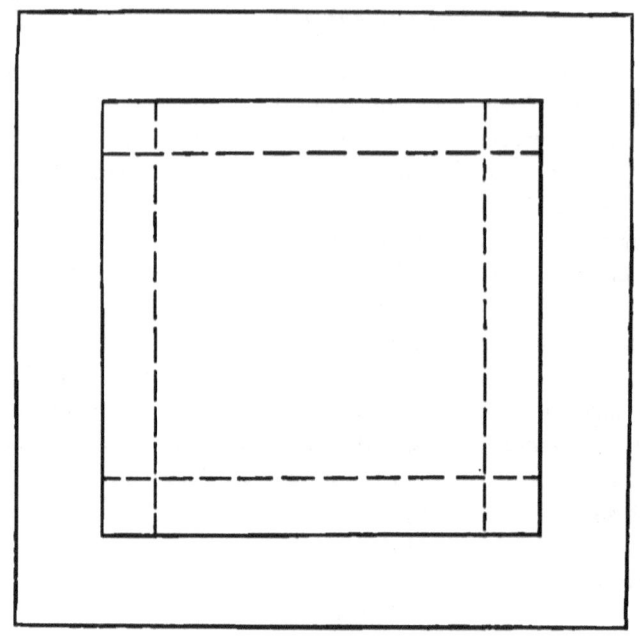

Fig. 27.— Representing a hole in a garment.

Fig. 29.— Patch basted on, ready for stitching.

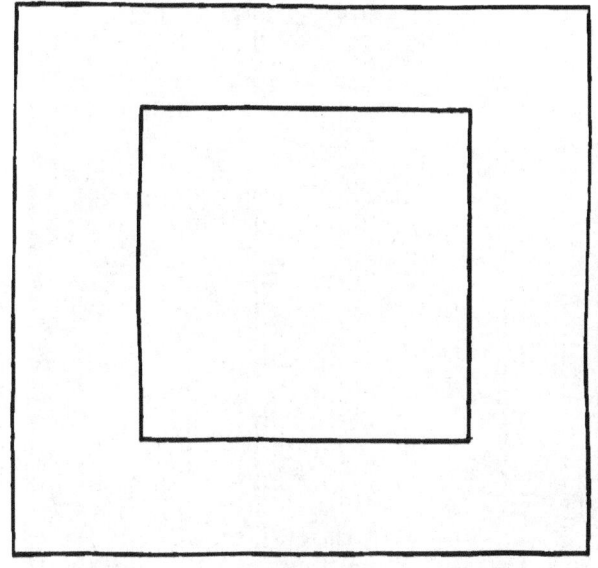

Fig. 31. — Patch completed, showing right side.

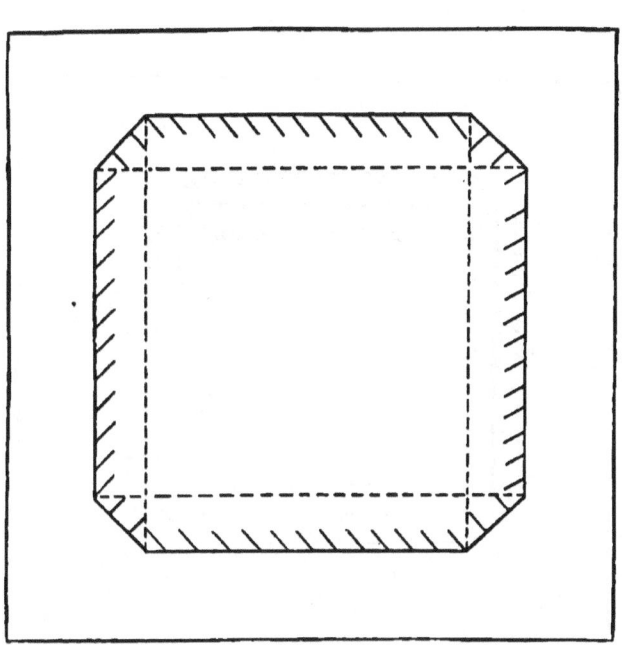

Fig. 30. — Patch stitched in and overcast.

Fig. 33.—Oversewed patch. Upper or right side.

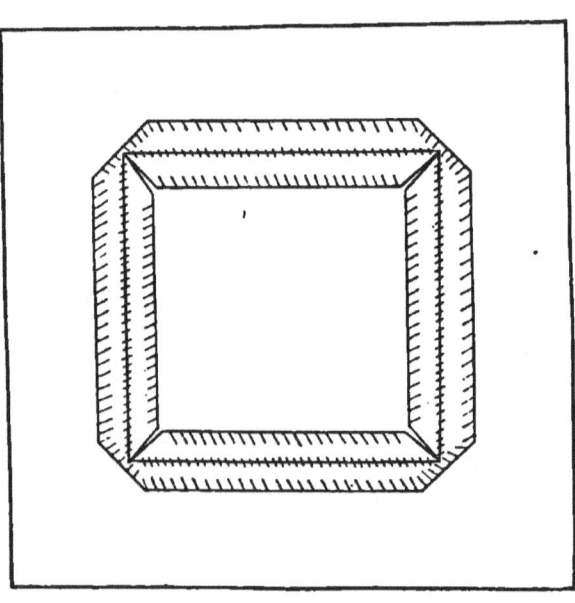

Fig. 32.—Oversewed patch. Under or wrong side.

SECOND YEAR'S SEWING. 39

52. How is a gusset cut? *Ans.* Cut a piece of cloth 1¼ in. square, cut off ¾ in. diagonally from one corner (Figs. 34, 35, 36, 37, 38).

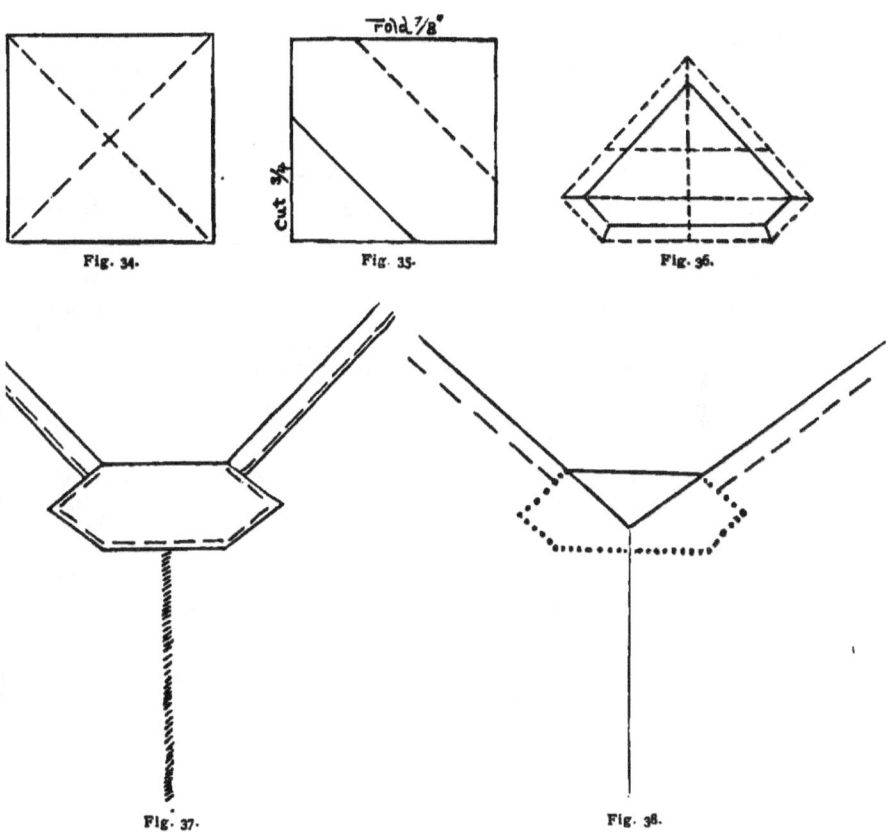

Fig. 34.   Fig. 35.   Fig. 36.

Fig. 37.   Fig. 38.

Method of preparing and sewing in a gusset.

53. How is a gusset sewed in? *Ans.* Place the apex of the triangle at the end of the seam. Oversew to the cloth ½ in. on each side,

beginning at the apex. The remaining part is folded over on the under side of the work, carefully basted to lie smooth, and hemmed down (see Figs. 37, 38).

54. Why does a gusset make the seam stronger? *Ans.* A gusset makes the seam stronger because its folded edge is on the bias, and if it is strongly sewed at the corners, it is impossible to tear it.

55. How is a tuck made? *Ans.* A tuck is made by folding the cloth straight by a thread from edge to edge, and basting this fold at the desired width. A running seam close below the basting finishes the tuck.

56. How are the stitches made in basting for a tuck? *Ans.* The basting stitches are made one inch long for a tuck.

57. How long are the spaces between? *Ans.* The spaces between are $\frac{1}{8}$ in. long.

58. Why should the stitches be longer than in basting an ordinary seam? *Ans.* The basting stitches should be longer for a tuck because they make a better guide for the running stitches, which must be very straight.

59. How is the thread joined in running tucks? *Ans.* In running tucks make a tied knot that can be easily concealed between the folds of the tuck three stitches back.

60. What is the use of a tuck? *Ans.* A tuck is used for ornament, or in order that the garment may be lengthened at some future time by letting it down.

61. What is gathering? *Ans.* Gathering is making a line of running stitches, and drawing the thread so as to full or gather the cloth (Fig. 39, A and B).

62. What should always be done before gathering? *Ans.* The edge should be marked in halves and quarters by colored cross-stitches (see Fig. 41, A).

63. What should always be done after gathering? *Ans.* After gathering, the gathers should be stroked or laid.
64. How is the stroking done? *Ans.* For stroking, the gathers must be pushed close together on the thread, and the loose end of the thread

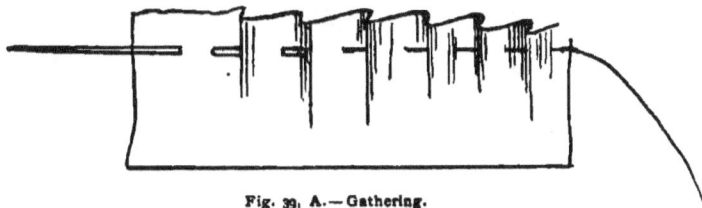

Fig. 39, A.—Gathering.

fastened firmly about a pin set at the end of the running, so that it cannot slip. Then the work is held between the thumb and first finger of the left hand, the thumb being directly over the gathering thread; and with a large needle or pin in the right hand, work-

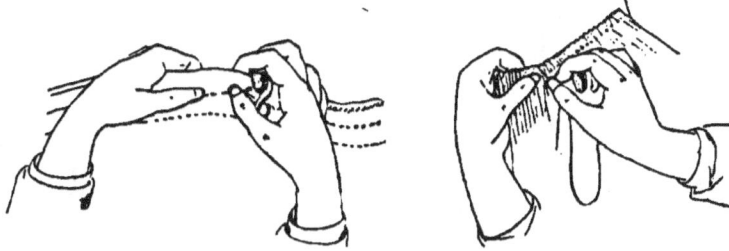

Fig. 39, B.—Running.   Fig. 40.—Gathers stroked or laid.

ing from left to right, each gather is pressed separately under the left thumb, while the pin strokes down a short distance between it and the next gather (Fig. 40). Then turn the work and stroke above the gathering stitches in the same way, but never so violently as to make a scratching sound with the needle.

65. How is a gathered piece of cloth prepared for sewing to a band, or binding? *Ans.* In preparing gathers for sewing to a band, find the middle of the band, and mark it with a line of small basting stitches (see Fig. 41, B); pin the middle of the band to the middle

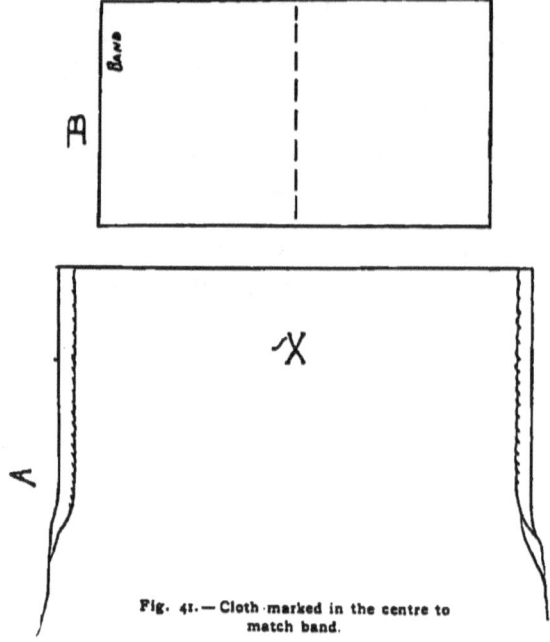

Fig. 41.—Cloth marked in the centre to match band.

of the gathered piece. Then pin the ends of the gathered piece to the same edge ⅛ in. from the ends of the band. This ⅛ in. of the band is left to turn in, to finish the ends. Then place the gathers evenly in each half of the band, and baste the gathered piece and band together, holding the gathers toward the person (Fig. 42).

SECOND YEAR'S SEWING. 43

66. How should gathers be sewed to a band? *Ans.* Fasten the ends of the band securely to the gathered piece by oversewing together the edge of the gathered piece and band from the right and left top corners down to the line of gathers; here take three oversewing stitches. (If this is done securely, the garment will wear out before the band rips at the ends.) Now, holding the gathers toward the sewer, make a back-stitch over each gather. The basting is then taken out. Now turn the band up from the gathers, crease, and

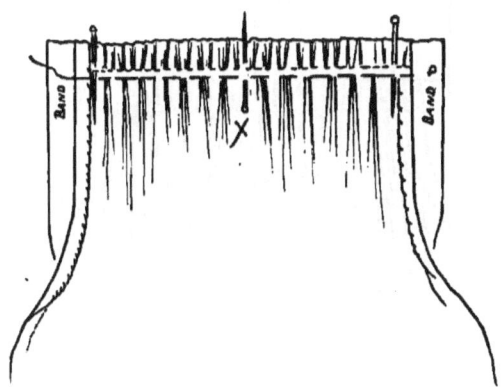

Fig. 42.—Cloth basted to the band.

baste the band in position of Fig. 43; turn in, baste, and oversew the ends of the band, the loose side of which, having been turned over $\frac{1}{8}$ in., must be pinned down over the line of stitching. Then baste and hem it down. In hemming down this edge of the band, take up one gather in each stitch (Fig. 44).

67. How should a buttonhole be cut? *Ans.* A buttonhole should be cut in double cloth, the end generally $\frac{1}{4}$ in. from the edge of the cloth, and as long as the diameter of the button.

68. What is the first thing to be done to a buttonhole after cutting it?

Ans. The buttonhole should be overcast immediately after being cut.

69. Where is the overcasting of a buttonhole begun? *Ans.* Begin to overcast a buttonhole at the lower left-hand end.

70. How is a buttonhole overcast? *Ans.* To overcast a buttonhole, hold

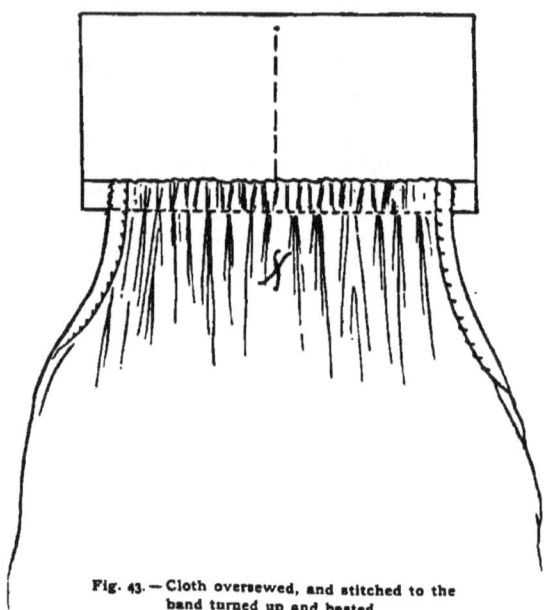

Fig. 43.—Cloth oversewed, and stitched to the band turned up and basted.

it lengthwise of the left forefinger, keeping that pointed to the right, and having the folded edge of the cloth toward the wrist. Then begin at the lower left-hand corner and overcast the left-hand side. Then turn the buttonhole, bring the folded edge to the end of the finger, and overcast the right-hand side (see Fig. 45); then back in cross-stitches to the outer end of the buttonhole. Here make a

SECOND YEAR'S SEWING.   45

cross-bar by overcasting one stitch to the right, and then one stitch to the left, until three cross-stitches have been made. (This makes

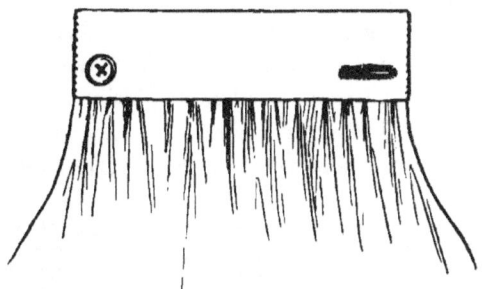

Fig. 44. — Band finished.

a round, strong outer end to the buttonhole when worked.) Now cross-stitch the left-hand side back to the starting-point (Fig. 46).

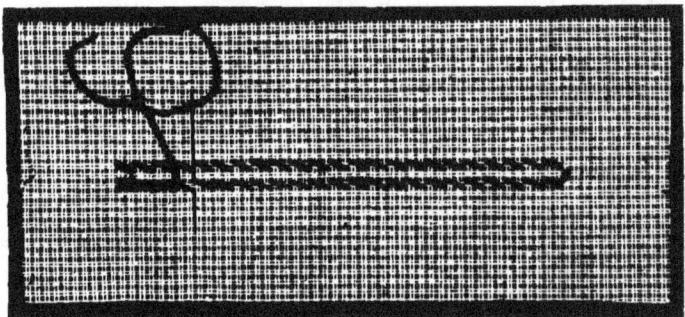

Fig. 45. — Overcasting the right-hand side, making cross-stitches.

Then put the needle through to the under side, take one running stitch, and cut the thread. See buttonhole in canvas sampler.

Represent on the blackboard the different steps of preparing and the way of holding a buttonhole.

71. How is a buttonhole worked? *Ans.* From the lower left-hand corner to the lower right-hand corner, then a straight bar is made across the lower or inner end.
72. How should the buttonhole stitch be made? *Ans.* In making a buttonhole stitch, the needle is put through the cloth, as for the overcasting, at the lower left-hand corner, then the thread from the eye of the needle is brought around the point of the needle from right to left, and the needle pulled through, bringing the loop up

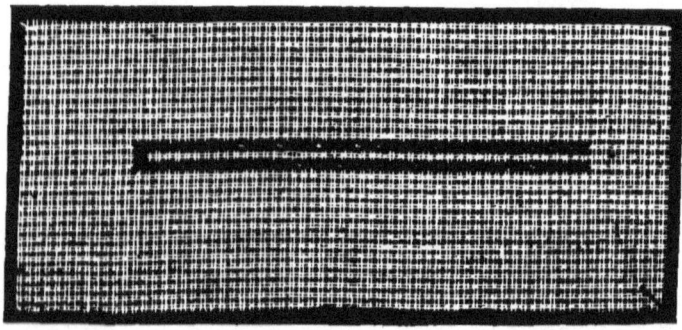

Fig. 46.—Buttonhole overcast twice.

straight, care being taken that it passes over the other end of the thread. The stitches should be made very near together, especially at the round end.

73. How should the straight bar be made at the lower end? *Ans.* Draw the worked edges together by making four stitches, one over the other, across the lower end of the buttonhole, then, beginning at the right-hand side, make five buttonhole stitches covering these, the middle stitch directly in the middle between the two sides of the buttonhole.

Draw these steps in buttonhole making on the blackboard.

SECOND YEAR'S SEWING. 47

74. Where should the button be sewed on? *Ans.* The button should be sewed on the other end of the band from the buttonhole, directly

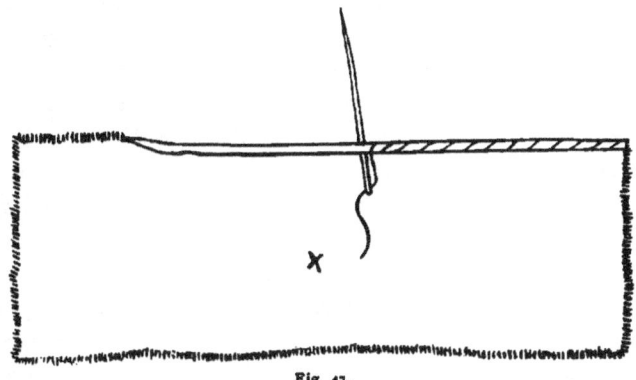

Fig. 47.

opposite the buttonhole, the edge of the button being a little inside of the edge of the band.

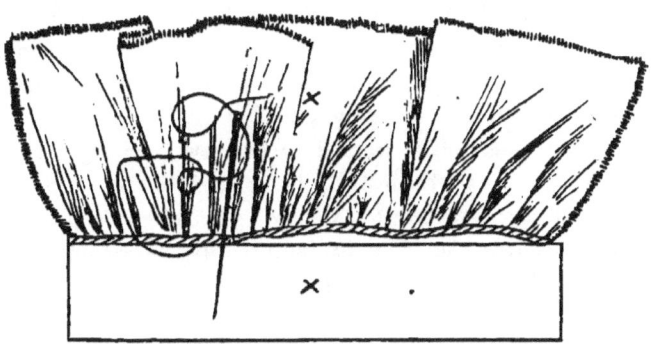

Fig. 48.

75. How should the button be sewed on? *Ans.* To sew on the button, the thread should be doubled, and a tied knot made in the end;

then the needle put through the cloth from the right or upper side, leaving the knot where the button is to be sewed. Then put the needle up through the cloth and one hole in the button and down through an opposite hole until the needle goes through a little hard, then bring the needle up between the button and the cloth and wind the thread three times around the thread there, to stem the button, and then fasten the thread on the wrong side.

76. How is the whipping done? *Ans.* After cutting the edge evenly by one thread and marking with a cross-stitch the half and quarters, the edge of the ruffle is rolled under in a small, hard roll, on the wrong side between the thumb and first finger of the left hand, one inch at a time, and stitches like hemming stitches are made over it, except that the needle is put up under the roll and brought out at the top of the roll (Fig. 47). At every fifth stitch the thread is held firmly, and the ruffle is fulled as on a gathering thread.

77. How is this ruffle sewed to the sampler? *Ans.* Pin the middle of the ruffle to the middle of the band; holding the sampler toward the person, oversew the ruffle to the band, sewing from left to right in order to make one stitch come in every little groove made by the whipping (see Fig. 48).

Although the pupils have learned to oversew from right to left, the teacher should tell them that, in some kinds of work, a better effect will be produced by sewing from left to right; as, overcasting woollens that fray or ravel easily, oversewing a whipped ruffle to a band, herringbone stitch, etc.

CHAPTER III.

Third Year's Sewing.

In the third year the sampler is made of fine white cotton. For this and the work of succeeding years on bleached cotton, the yard wide Fitchville or Masonville cloths have been found most desirable for handsewing, being without dressing. During the first five months of this year, fifteen minutes of the first hour should be devoted to button-hole making with fine cotton, Nos. 50, 60, and 70, and silk twist. The teacher should have in readiness pieces of canvas and flannel, 3 in. × 8 in., on which to teach cross-stitch, herringbone, and feather-stitch, also pieces of linen, to teach hemstitching upon. For several months give class instruction of one-half hour each month in these stitches, as all this kind of work will be used in making the white cloth sampler.

In order to train the eyes and hands of pupils, that they may be prepared for advanced work, let them now practise in cutting exactly along the lines of striped and checked cloths, material for which can be found in pieces left over from dressmaking in the sixth class.

The class drill should be reviewed as often as practicable.

Letters of the alphabet may be made in cross-stitch (see Fig. 49). This practice is to train the eye and hand in spacing distance by threads both across and lengthwise of the cloth, and for marking the initials and age on the sampler. Its practical value otherwise is small, and too much time should not be given to it. Outline-stitch can be used for initials and age, if a pupil's eyesight is too delicate to count threads.

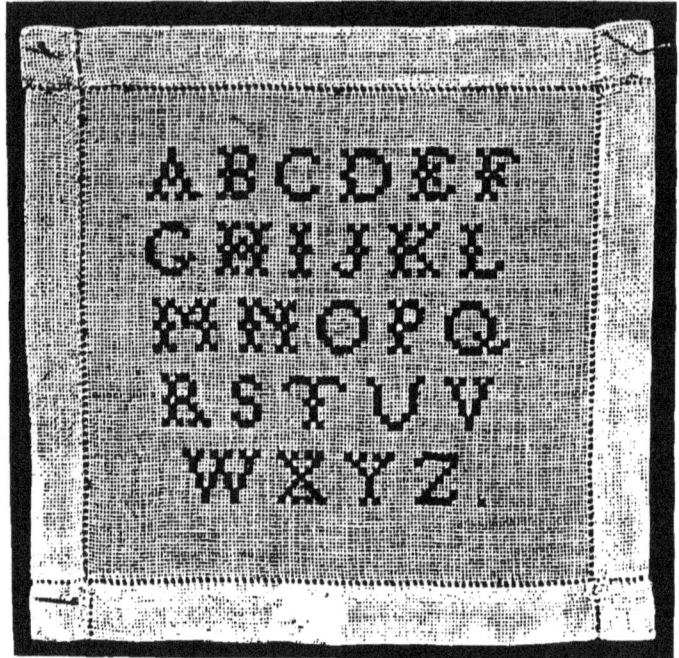

Fig. 49.

SAMPLER No. 3.

MATERIALS REQUIRED.

Two strips of bleached cotton (with selvedge on one side) 18 in. × 5 in.
Two strips of cotton (lengthwise, without selvedge) 9½ in. × 5 in.
Three pieces of cotton (for patches) 3 in. square.
One piece of cotton (for band) 3½ in. × 2 in.

THIRD YEAR'S SEWING.

One piece of cotton (for gusset) 1¼ in. square.
One piece of cotton, cut bias, ¾ in. wide and 10 in. long (for facing the narrow ruffle).
One strip of Lonsdale cotton (across the cloth) 18½ in. × 5 in
One strip of Lonsdale cotton (across the cloth) 14 in. × 2¼ in
One strip of flannel (even threads) lengthwise, 18 in. × 6 in.
One piece of crash (even threads) for pocket, 6¼ in. × 4½ in.
White spool cotton Nos. 40, 50, 60, 70, 90, and 100.
Needles Nos. 9, 10, 11, 12.
Fine crewel needle.
One needleful of white buttonhole twist.
Three spools (three yards each) of embroidery silk in some color.
One shirt button.
One large pearl button.
The estimated cost of white cotton sampler is thirty cents.

DIRECTIONS FOR MAKING SAMPLER.

I.

Baste together selvedges of the first two strips of cloth and oversew with No. 60 cotton and No. 10 needle, leaving a distance of 4 in. open at one end for a gusset; open the seam and press flat with the thumb-nail.

II.

Turn a narrow "handkerchief hem" on the raw edge of the first strip of cloth, as shown in illustration, and hem with No. 70 cotton and No. 10 needle.

III.

6½ in. from the bottom edge of the strip cut a small hole, as shown in illustration, and mend the hole by making a hemmed-on patch, using a No. 10 needle and No. 70 cotton.

IV.

3½ in. above this patch cut another hole, and mend it by inserting a stitched-in patch, using No. 60 cotton and No. 9 needle for stitching, and No. 70 cotton and No. 10 needle for overcasting.

V.

Join by a French seam (for direction see second year) the two strips 9½ in. × 5 in.; join on widths, making strip No. 3 18 in. long.

VI.

6 in. above the bottom edge of this strip make a cut having two right angles, in this shape ⌐⌐, and darn it according to questions and answers 10 to 16.

VII.

2 in. above the French seam cut a hole and mend with an oversewed patch, using No. 60 cotton and No. 10 needle for the oversewing, and No. 70 cotton and No. 10 needle for overcasting.

VIII.

Join strip No. 3 to the raw edge of strip No. 2, making a fell, as described in sampler No. 2; use No. 50 cotton and No. 9 needle for stitching, No. 60 cotton and No. 9 needle for hemming. When felling a bias seam, lay the hem with the grain of the cloth. It is much easier to hem with the grain than against it (Fig. 50).

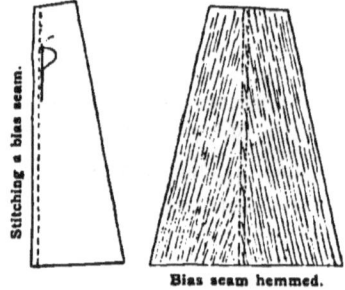

Bias seam hemmed.
Fig. 50.

IX.

On the lower edge of the sampler turn a hem 2½ in. broad, and hem with No. 70 cotton and No. 10 needle.

X.

Make a buttonhole 1 in. long in the broad hem of strip No. 3; use No. 70 cotton and No. 10 needle for overcasting, and No. 50 cotton and No. 9 needle for working the buttonhole. Make a buttonhole 1 in. long in the broad hem of strip No. 1.

XI.

Put in a gusset at the opening of the oversewed seam, using No. 60 cotton and No. 10 needle for oversewing, and No. 70 cotton and No. 10 needle for hemming.

XII.

Gather strip No. 1, $\frac{1}{4}$ in. below the top, stroke, and put into the band, using No. 50 cotton and No. 9 needle for gathering and stitching, No. 60 cotton and No. 9 needle for oversewing and hemming.

Make a buttonhole $\frac{1}{2}$ in. long in the right-hand end of the band.

Sew a shirt button on the left-hand end of the band, using No. 50 cotton and No. 9 needle.

XIII.

Take the smaller strip of Lonsdale and make a handkerchief hem on each end and across one side, using No. 100 cotton and No. 12 needle. This is for a ruffle.

Gather the ruffle $\frac{1}{4}$ in. from the raw edge; stroke and stitch to the top of the sampler with No. 60 cotton and No. 10 needle. Still holding the ruffle toward the person, baste to this seam the bias strip of cloth, and make one back-stitch and two running stitches directly over the gathering. Turn all these edges flat to the under edge of the sampler; turn under the top edge and one end of the bias strip; hem the turned edge to the sampler and oversew one end. The other end is held in place by the stitching of the flannel.

XIV.

Make a handkerchief hem on the ends of the second piece of Lonsdale, then make a ¼ in. hem on one side of it. Above this hem make three tucks the same width as the hem, using No. 90 cotton and No. 11 needle.

Whip the upper edge of the ruffle, using No. 40 cotton and No. 9 needle.

Oversew this ruffle to the lower edge of the sampler, holding the sampler toward the person, sewing from left to right, so as to make one stitch come in every little groove made by the whipping. Use No. 50 cotton and No. 9 needle.

XV.

Turn down one end of the flannel strip 1¼ in., baste it, and then make herringbone stitch over the edge with embroidery silk, using the crewel needle (see question and answer 32).

Hold the flannel so that the herringbone stitches just made will be at the right-hand side and on the under side of the flannel; then turn down and baste the upper edge of the flannel ⅛ in., turn again 1 in., and baste for a hem. Then blind-stitch this hem with No. 9 needle and No. 60 cotton, according to question and answer 33.

With embroidery silk, feather-stitch over the edge of this hem, according to question and answer 35.

Measure the strip of flannel with the raw edge of the sampler, and with a pencil draw scallops on the end so as to make it the same length as the sampler when finished (see question and answer 36). Then, with embroidery silk, work as described in question and answer 37.

3 in. above the scalloping make a cut in the flannel 1½ in. long, and darn, using No. 100 cotton and No. 12 needle for overcasting the

cut edges together, and No. 8 needle and ravellings of flannel for darning.

Half way between the darn and the top of the flannel strip cut a hole and mend it with a patch, according to question and answer 38.

In the hem of the flannel strip, cut a buttonhole 1 in. long, overcast with No. 70 cotton and No. 10 needle, and work with buttonhole twist.

Baste the flannel to the raw edge of the sampler ¼ in. from the edge, and stitch with No. 50 cotton and No. 9 needle, holding the flannel toward the person.

XVI.

Prepare and hemstitch the pocket according to questions and answers 40 to 48.

A buttonhole is cut in the middle of the hem of the pocket, and overcast with No. 70 cotton and No. 10 needle, and worked with No. 40 cotton and No. 9 needle.

The initials are to be worked in the centre of the pocket, ½ in. below the hemstitching; work with embroidery silk, in cross-stitch or outline-stitch (see questions and answers 50 to 53). The age is worked in the same way, below the initials.

A row of double feather-stitching is made around the pocket, at the option of the pupil.

The pocket is basted to the centre of the sampler and hemmed on with No. 60 cotton and No. 9 needle.

XVII.

A stay is placed on the wrong side of the sampler (see questions and answers 56 to 58), where the button is to be sewed on. This is hemmed with No. 70 cotton and No. 10 needle.

The button is sewed on with No. 50 cotton and No. 9 needle (white cloth sampler, Fig. 51).

Fig. 51.—Sampler No. 3.

QUESTIONS AND ANSWERS.

1. What number cotton and needle are used for all bastings on this sampler? *Ans.* No. 50 cotton and No. 9 needle are used for basting on the white sampler.
2. What seam is made first on the bleached or white cloth sampler? *Ans.* On the bleached sampler the oversewed seam is made first.
3. What number cotton and what number needle are used for the oversewing? *Ans.* No. 60 cotton and No. 10 needle are used for the oversewing.
4. For hemming the sampler, what cotton and needle are used? *Ans.* For hemming the sampler, No. 70 cotton and No. 10 needle are used.
5. For sewing the hemmed-on patch, what cotton and what needle are used? *Ans.* For sewing a hemmed-on patch, No. 70 cotton and No. 10 needle are used.
6. For sewing the stitched-in patch, what cotton and what needle are used? *Ans.* For stitching the patch, No. 60 cotton and a No. 9 needle are used; and No. 70 cotton and No. 10 needle for the overcasting.
7. What number cotton and what number needle are used for the first part of the French seam? *Ans.* No. 60 cotton and No. 9 needle are used for the first part of the French seam.
8. What number cotton and what number needle are used for stitching the French seam? *Ans.* For stitching the French seam, No. 50 cotton and No. 9 needle are used.
9. For the oversewed patch, what cotton and what needle are used? *Ans.* No. 60 cotton and a No. 10 needle are used for oversewing the patch, and No. 70 cotton and No. 10 needle for overcasting it.
10. How should a torn or cut place be prepared for darning? *Ans.* The edges of the cut or tear should be caught together as evenly as

possible by fine overcasting on the wrong side, particular care being taken at the corners (Fig. 52); then, a straight line of basting stitches should be made all around the tear, ¼ inch from the joined edges, to mark where the lines of darning end (Fig. 53).

11. What number cotton and what number needle are used for the darn on the sampler? *Ans.* No. 100 cotton and No. 12 needle are used for the darning on the sampler.

Show this preparation for darning on the blackboard.

12. How is the torn place darned after being prepared in this way? *Ans.* Straight lines of fine stitches are made back and forth from

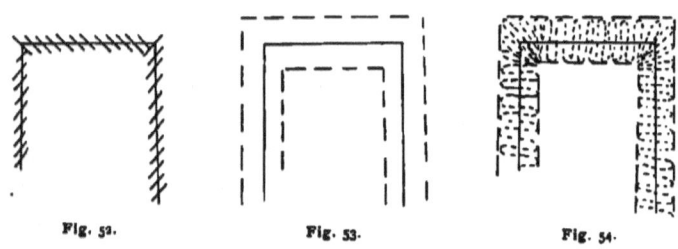

Fig. 52.   Fig. 53.   Fig. 54.

one guiding basting to the other, leaving a very small loop at each turning. (See canvas sampler, Fig. 54.)

13. How are the corners darned? *Ans.* The lines of running stitches are made slanting instead of straight, so that they all come together at the corner of the inside basting. (Illustrate on the blackboard.)

14. Why are the little loops left? *Ans.* The little loops are left to allow for drawing or shrinking. (Represent such a darn on the blackboard.)

15. Is the basting left in after the darning is finished? *Ans.* No; the bastings are cut at every third or fourth stitch and carefully drawn out.

THIRD YEAR'S SEWING.

16. Should a darn be made on the right or the wrong side of the cloth? *Ans.* Generally, a darn should be on the wrong side of the cloth.
17. What number cotton and what number needle are used for stitching the fell? *Ans.* For stitching the fell, No. 50 cotton and No. 9 needle are used.
18. For hemming the fell, what cotton and needle are used? *Ans.* For hemming the fell, No. 60 cotton and No. 9 needle are used.
19. For overcasting buttonholes, what cotton and what needle are used? *Ans.* For overcasting buttonholes, No. 70 cotton and No. 10 needle are used.
20. For working buttonholes, what cotton and what needle are used? *Ans.* For working buttonholes, No. 50 cotton and No. 9 needle are used.
21. What number cotton and what number needle are used for the gusset on the sampler? *Ans.* For sewing a gusset on the sampler, No. 60 cotton and No. 10 needle are used for oversewing, No. 70 cotton and No. 10 needle for hemming.
22. What number cotton and what number needle are used for gathering? *Ans.* For gathering, No. 50 cotton and No. 9 needle are used.
23. For stitching gathers into a band, what cotton and what needle are used? *Ans.* For stitching gathers into a band, No. 50 cotton and No. 9 needle are used.
24. For hemming the band down and oversewing the ends, what cotton and what needle are used? *Ans.* For hemming and oversewing the band, No. 60 cotton and No. 9 needle are used.
25. For sewing the button on the band, what cotton and what needle are used? *Ans.* For sewing the button on the band, No. 50 cotton and No. 9 needle are used.
26. For hemming cambric ruffles, what cotton and what needle are used? *Ans.* For hemming cambric ruffles, No. 100 cotton and No. 12 needle are used.

27. What is a ruffle? *Ans.* A ruffle is a strip of cloth gathered on one edge and hemmed on the other, which is then sewed to a plain piece of cloth.*

28. What is the use of a ruffle? *Ans.* A ruffle is used to trim, and sometimes to lengthen a garment.

29. What number cotton and what number needle are used for gathering the narrow ruffle? *Ans.* For gathering the narrow ruffle, No. 50 cotton and No. 9 needle are used.

30. For stitching the ruffled piece to the plain piece, what cotton and what needle are used? *Ans.* For stitching on the ruffled piece, No. 50 cotton and No. 9 needle are used.

31. What needle and cotton are used for sewing the bias facing to the narrow ruffle? *Ans.* No. 60 cotton and No. 9 needle for the stitching part; No. 10 needle and No. 70 cotton for the hemming part.

✓ 32. How is herringbone or cat-stitch made? *Ans.* A knot is made in the thread and the needle is brought up from the under side of the work, at the point nearest the person, as this stitch is usually worked upward or from the worker; it is sometimes worked from left to right. The work is held over the first finger of the left hand, kept in place with the second finger and thumb. The thread is first drawn through, then the needle is put through $\frac{1}{8}$ in. to the right and $\frac{1}{4}$ in. above and brought up again $\frac{1}{8}$ in. below perpendicularly, care being taken to keep the thread at the left of the needle. The needle is next put through $\frac{1}{8}$ in. to the left and $\frac{1}{4}$ in. above, and the stitch made in the same manner, keeping the thread to

---

* When gathering a ruffle with a raw edge for a heading, always gather on the under or wrong side. When gathering a ruffle with a finished heading, or a dress skirt, gather on the upper or right side, beginning on the right-hand end, for both upper and under side. Then the long end of the gathering thread will be at the left end of the part gathered, and the work can be easily drawn into place.

the right of the needle. The third stitch is to the left and above, as before (Fig. 55).

33. How is a hem blind-stitched? *Ans.* A hem is blind-stitched by catching the under part of the first fold down to the single cloth below it, with running stitches, so that no stitches show on the upper side.

34. What stitch is used to ornament the hem after blind-stitching it? *Ans.* To ornament the hem, feather or vine stitching is used.

35. How is feather or vine stitch made? *Ans.* A knot is made in the thread, and the needle is brought up from the under side of the

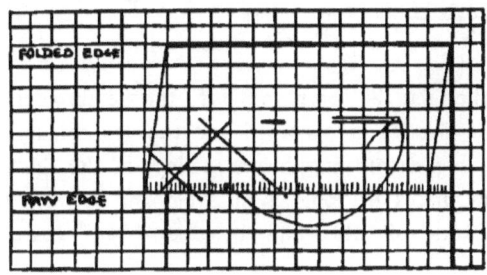

Fig. 55.

work, at the point farthest from the person, as feather-stitch is always worked downward or toward the worker. The work is held over the first finger of the left hand, kept in place with the second finger and thumb. The thread is drawn through, then placed under the thumb while the next stitch is taken; the needle is put through to the under side $\frac{1}{8}$ in. to the right and a trifle below the place where it was brought up, and brought up again $\frac{1}{8}$ in. perpendicularly; the thread is drawn through until caught in the loop formed by the thread held under the thumb. The next stitch is made in the same manner $\frac{1}{8}$ in. to the left and a trifle below, the third stitch to the right and below, and so on. This is the simplest form of feather-stitch, which may be varied in many ways, as shown by the illustrations (Figs. 56 to 57).

In describing the so-called "buttonhole stitch" of embroidery, it is spoken of as an embroidery edge stitch, so that the child may not associate it with buttonholes, and be tempted, by the ease of making, to use it for them.

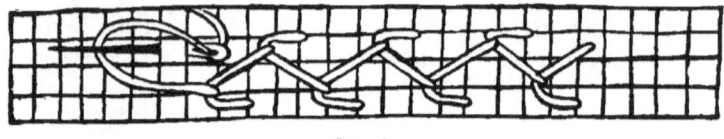

Fig. 56.

36. How is the flannel prepared for the embroidery edge stitch? *Ans.* The flannel is prepared for the embroidery edge stitch by first marking out on card-board scallops of the required size. Draw a straight line 3 in. long, $\frac{1}{2}$ in. from the lower edge of the card-board. Mark off this line by dots 1 in. apart, and half way

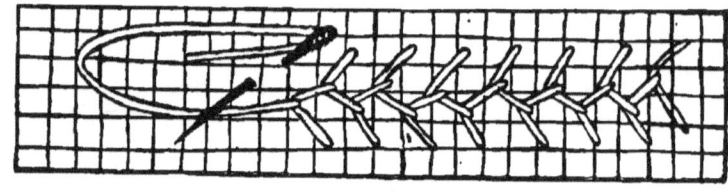

Fig. 57.

between each two make a dot on the lower edge of the card-board. Connect these dots by half circles and cut them out with the scissors. Then lay the card-board evenly on the edge of the cloth, and mark the scallops on it with a lead pencil, holding the side of the pencil with care perpendicularly against the edge of the card-board. Then, making a dot on the cloth just $\frac{1}{8}$ in. above the centre of the curve in each scallop, connect the ends of each outside curve by a line drawn through this point. This marks out the space covered by the stitches. With fine darning or tambour cotton make running stitches on the lines marked out, to strengthen the edge.

37. How is the embroidery edge stitch made? *Ans.* Fasten the thread, to begin the embroidery edge stitch, by taking two or three running stitches between the two curves of the scallop, and bring the needle up at the left-hand point of the first scallop, just on the lower edge of the lower curve, holding the edge toward the person. Then hold the thread down with the left thumb, and put the needle through to the lower side on the upper edge of the upper curve, just over this point, and bring it up again on the lower edge of the lower curve, close to where it came up at first, and over the thread held down by the thumb. The stitch is then tightened by drawing the thread downward. This is repeated, taking care to keep the stitches as close as possible. The central stitch of the scallop should be $\frac{1}{8}$ in. long and vertical, the others should shorten and slope gradually to each end.

38. How is a patch made in flannel? *Ans.* To mend a hole in flannel, a square piece of the material with the edges cut even (not turned in) is basted over the worn or torn place and on the wrong side; this is herringbone-stitched very finely all around the edges, using No. 10 needle and No. 100 cotton. The worn place is then cut out square, and the even edge herringbone-stitched, in the same manner, to the patch (see Figs. 58, 59).

39. Why are the edges of the patch not turned under, as in making a similar patch on cloth? *Ans.* Because turned edges in flannel are clumsy and unnecessary, as the material will not ravel when held by the herringbone stitches.

40. Of what material is the pocket of the sampler made? *Ans.* The pocket on the sampler is made of crash.

Fig. 59.—Flannel patch finished, showing upper or right side.

Fig. 58.—Flannel patch herringboned to the under side.

41. How is the pocket cut? *Ans.* Cut by a thread a piece of crash for the pocket 6½ in. × 4½ in.
42. What is the first step in preparing the hem for hemstitching? *Ans.* To prepare for the hemstitched hem, draw six threads across the crash 3 in. from the end.
43. What is the next step in preparing the pocket? *Ans.* After drawing the threads for the hemstitching, turn the edge of the piece of crash down ¼ in. and baste them with No. 40 cotton and No. 8 needle.
44. What is the second step in preparing the hem? *Ans.* The second step in preparing the hem is to fold it down and baste it so that the edge of the fold already made lies evenly along the upper edge of the space left by the drawn threads.
45. How is the hemstitching done? *Ans.* To begin the hemstitching, make a tied knot in the thread and take two or three running stitches on the under side of the fold, then bring the needle to the lower side at the left-hand edge. Now, holding the work over the first finger of the left hand, the hem toward the person, hold the left thumb over the thread and put the needle down between the fourth and fifth threads, take up the four threads to the left, bring the needle up, and pull the loop thus made close to the edge of the hem. Holding the thread firmly under the left thumb, take an edging stitch over the edge of the hem close to the right of the four threads just taken up. Then take up four more threads and repeat. Always work on the side on which the hem is turned, and from left to right (Fig. 60, A, B).
46. How is the thread joined in hemstitching? *Ans.* Tie a knot in the fresh thread. Draw the needle through the upper fold of the hem, two stitches back, working over these stitches, and proceed as before.
47. What number needle and what number thread are used in hemstitching the pocket? *Ans.* In hemstitching the pocket, No. 60 cotton and No. 9 needle are used.

48. How should the ends of the hem be finished? *Ans.* The ends of the hem should be oversewed; it is better to do this before the hemstitching, as it sometimes prevents unequal stretching.

49. What number cotton and what number needle are used for the buttonhole on the pocket? *Ans.* For this buttonhole, No. 70 cotton and No. 10 needle are used for overcasting, and No. 9 needle and No. 40 cotton in making the buttonhole stitch.

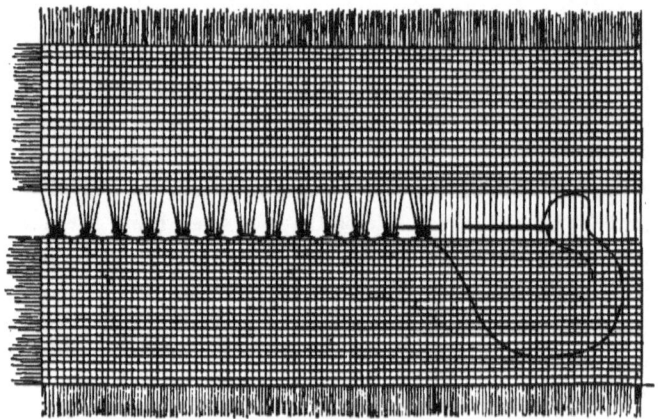

Fig. 60, A.—Hemstitching.

50. How are the letters made on the pocket? *Ans.* To begin the marking stitch, the needle is brought through to the upper side at the place for beginning the letter, the end of the thread being held on the under side until secured by the first stitch. The stitch is made by putting the needle through to the lower side two threads to the right and two threads upward (in marking on canvas or coarse crash) and bringing it up two threads below, perpendicularly. This makes the under half of the stitch. Next, the needle is put through to the lower side two threads upward and two threads to

the left, bringing the thread diagonally across the lower half of the stitch and completing it. The pupil can see, from the letter she is copying, where the needle should be brought up to begin the next stitch, which is made in the same way. After finishing the first initial, four threads are left and a period made with a single cross-stitch. Leave four threads and begin the next initial, and so on.

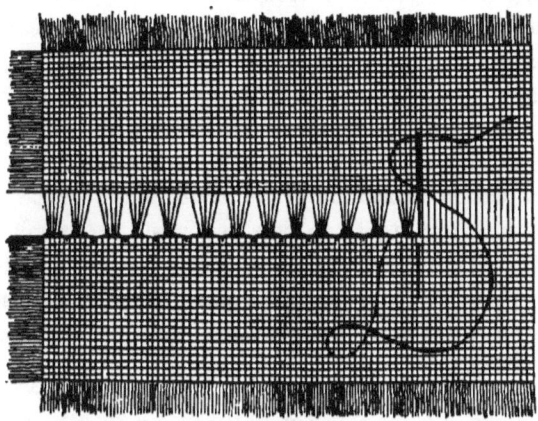

Fig. 60, B.— Hemstitching.

51. How should the thread be fastened in finishing? *Ans.* The thread should be run between the stitch and the canvas on the under side, for the length of three stitches, and cut off with the scissors.
52. In what direction should the letters be worked? *Ans.* In marking, the letters should be made from left to right.
53. How is the place to begin lettering the pocket to be found? *Ans.* To find the place of the first marking stitch, count the number of stitches necessary for all the initials, the periods, and the spaces between, then $\frac{1}{2}$ in. below the hemstitching, count from the

middle of the pocket half this number of stitches to the left, and this gives the place for the first stitch of the first initial.

54. How is the pocket sewed to the sampler? *Ans.* The pocket is hemmed to the sampler.
55. What number thread and what number needle are used for hemming on the pocket? *Ans.* To hem on the pocket, No. 60 thread and No. 9 needle are used.
56. Where should the button be sewed on? *Ans.* After the pocket is sewed on, lay the sampler flat on the desk and place a pin through the buttonhole and cloth beneath, $\frac{1}{8}$ in. from the top of the buttonhole; this gives the place where the button should be sewed.
57. Should the button be sewed on a single thickness of thin cloth? *Ans.* A button should never be sewed on a single thickness of thin cloth, where it has to bear any strain. A small square piece should be hemmed on under the place where the button belongs, to strengthen it. Now the white cloth sampler is finished.*
58. What is this small piece called? *Ans.* This small piece is called a stay.

NUMBER OF COTTON AND NUMBER OF NEEDLE FOR SAMPLER WORK.

	Cotton.	Needle.
Oversewed seam	60	10
French seam, run and back-stitched	60	9
French seam, stitched	50	9
Fell, stitched	50	9
Fell, hemmed	60	9
Hems, broad and narrow	70	10
Patch, hemmed on	70	10
Patch, stitched in	60	9

* The idea of the white cloth sampler originated with Miss Emma F. Ware, Milton, Mass. The one in use, here illustrated, has several alterations and additions.

THIRD YEAR'S SEWING.

	Cotton.	Needle.
Patch, overcast	70	10
Patch, oversewed	60	10
Darning	100	12
Gathering	50	9
Band, stitched on	50	9
Band, hemmed down and ends oversewed	60	9
Buttonholes, overcast	70	10
Buttonholes, worked	50	9
Button sewed on to band	50	9
Button sewed on for pocket	40	9
Lonsdale ruffles, hemmed	100	12
Narrow ruffles, gathered	50	9
Narrow ruffle, stitched on	60	10
Narrow ruffle, overcast	70	10
Tucks run in broad ruffle	90	11
Broad ruffle, whipped	40	9
Broad ruffle, oversewed on	50	9
Flannel, blind (or slip) stitched	60	9
Gusset, oversewed	60	10
Gusset, hemmed	70	10
Pocket, hemstitched	60	9
Pocket, buttonhole worked	40	9
Pocket, hemmed on	60	9
Stay for button, hemmed on	70	10
Flannel stitched on to sampler	50	9
Flannel overcast	70	10

CHAPTER IV.

Fourth Year's Sewing.

WHEN the fine white cotton sampler has not been finished in the third year, it must be completed as early as possible in the fourth year, to give the necessary time for advanced work.

The work laid out for this year includes advanced patching and darning on fine, plain, and figured woollens, heavy cloths, table linen, and silk, — the darning done with ravellings, fine worsted, linen and silk threads. Also stocking-darning.

Pupils of this year can cut and prepare all that is necessary in the sampler work for younger classes, such as cutting small paper patterns, cutting linen for pockets, lengths of flannel, and ruffles from the width of fine cambric. In this way they are learning to handle practically different kinds of cloth, to know thoroughly about the length, width, and bias of cloth, and why it should be cut certain ways for different purposes. They also gain the ability to use their hands rapidly and easily.

The class should study about different materials, such as wool, linen, and silk; explain how they are produced and how made into fabrics. If possible, show specimens in various stages from the raw product to the finished goods.

Patching: — I.

In patching, the pupil has been taught the importance of matching the patch with the cloth of the garment in the direction of the threads, figures, etc. In flannel the way of the nap, the selvedge, and the right and wrong sides of the cloth must be considered. As the edges of a flannel patch will not ravel, the raw edges can be herringboned to the under side of the cloth, and the raw edges of the cut can be neatly herringboned to the patch, as shown in Figs. 58, 59.

Fig. 61. — Patch hemmed to the right side.

Patching woollen dress material must be done according to the nature of the goods, the tear, etc., and judgment must be exercised in doing it. Sometimes more than one method may be wisely used. Four kinds of patches are described, viz. the hemmed-on (Fig. 61), the stitched-in, the oversewed, and the darned-on.

72 PROGRESSIVE LESSONS IN NEEDLEWORK.

II.

Darned-on patch:—

When a large patch is well matched to heavy cloth, it shows less than a small one. Darning is better than a small patch. A thread of the same color as the cloth should be used when patching and darning.

A darned-on patch is used for heavy cloths, especially in mending

Fig. 62.— Darned-on patch.

boys' trousers. If possible, use a patch of irregular edges, as when sewed down it is less noticeable than one with straight edges, and can, with care, often be made almost invisible (see Fig. 62).

By fine overcasting of cotton or silk secure the patch to the right side of the garment, the stitch being taken through the upper surface of the edge of the patch. This brings the upper surface of the patch nearly to the level of the cloth of the garment. Then the darning stitches should be taken below the surface of the patch and the garment, never showing on the top. To hide the turning at the end of the lines of darning, take a stitch diagonally (always under the surface) from the end stitch of the line finished to the place where the next line is to begin.

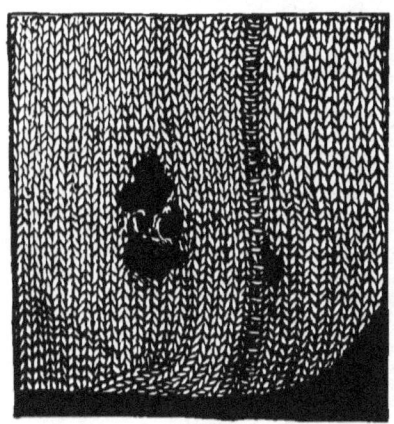
Fig. 63, A.

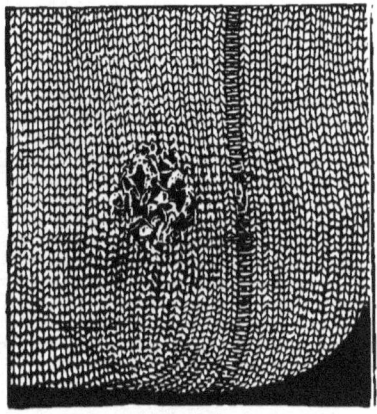
Fig. 63, B.

Pare off as little as possible of the ragged edges beneath, and catch them down securely to the under side of the patch with herringbone stitch so that the stitches do not show through.

The most important points of instruction are to consider the character of the cloth, the worn place, and the method of mending it.

III.

Darning:—

To darn a hole in a stocking (Fig. 63, A) or in woollen underclothing (if large), first draw the edges together as near as possible with fine cotton (Fig. 63, B); then make straight lines of darning between the two opposite sides of the hole, and leave a loop of the thread at the end of each line of turning, to allow for shrinking; darn across the hole in like manner at right angles to these lines (see Fig. 64). Each line of darning should begin 1 in. or more beyond the edge of the hole, and at

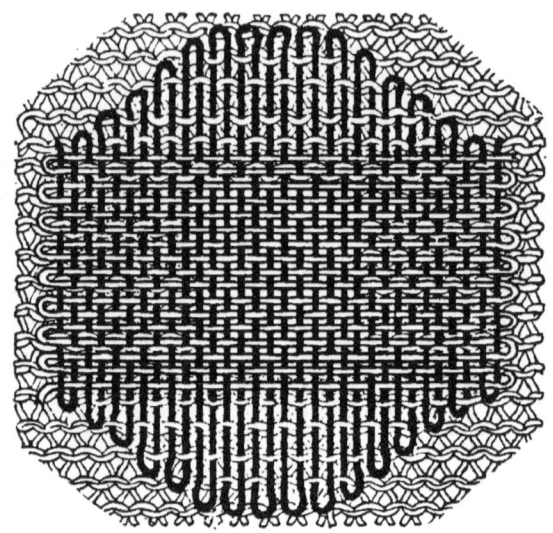

Fig. 64.

the left side of the worn or thin place. In one line pass the needle over the first thread and under the second, over the third and under the fourth, and so on, and in returning on the next line pass the needle over the threads taken up before, and under the threads left down (Fig. 64). (Illustrate on blackboard.)

If fine woollen thread is used in darning cotton stockings, the darn is much softer than when cotton thread is used. Care should always be taken when darning a worn place to make the lines of stitches of uneven length for the sake of strength. If the lines are of even length the whole strain is borne by one thread in the cloth, which soon gives way. Explain the different kinds of needles used for darning.

To show the necessity of darning before the hole actually appears, it should be explained that darning is a method of renewing the part of the cloth destroyed or weakened by wear, and in some cases is really hand-weaving. Thus, if the darning is over a thin place and not a hole, the work can be made stronger and less clumsy.

It would be well for the teacher to tell the child that, before stockings or woollen undergarments are washed, if a few stitches are taken with fine thread, drawing the torn edges evenly and as nearly together as possible, the hole instead of growing larger will full together at the edges and become smaller; thus the work of mending will be lessened, the mended garment will be stronger, and the mend itself is less conspicuous. Such information from a teacher is valuable for home use.

Fig. 65.—Darned with ravellings.

For darning woollen material, use a ravelling of the same if possible. Otherwise, use a fine worsted thread, splitting it if necessary and matching the color of the cloth (see Fig. 65).

In darning on silk or linen fabrics with fine floss, sewing silk, or ravellings of silk, the loops should be left shorter than in other darning, as the linen and silk threads do not shrink like cotton and wool threads.

IV.

Mexican work (Fig. 66),

As preliminary to general embroidery, is introduced in this grade. It gives a child valuable artistic training. Some children have natural gifts which are awakened and trained in this work in ways that are invaluable in after life. As a saving of school time, pupils may be allowed to take this work home and work on it there, when they show sufficient appreciation of neatness. It should be noticed that this primary Mexican work is practised in hemstitching and in herringbone stitch.

V.

Cutting:—

The scissors practice of the lower grades now becomes the wholly practical work of cutting patterns and garments. The pupils in this fourth year learn the use of the tape measure by measuring for patterns of plain undergarments. The measures are taken by the pupils on a child of the age and size to be fitted. These measures are written on the blackboard, where they are used in drawing a diagram according to the method explained in the class work. The pupil makes a similar diagram on paper.

Fig. 66.—Mexican work.

VI.

How to measure for drawers pattern:—

For the length, place the end of the tape measure at the waist line on the upper part of the hip, and measure to three inches below the knee. Draw the oblong 3 in. longer than that measurement, to allow for the upper slope (see scale of measurements). The width of the oblong is governed a little by the size of the pupil, and according to the teacher's judgment. 15 in. is the right width for an average size pupil of ten to fourteen years of age. For length of waistbands, pass the tape measure around the waist loosely; allow 2 in. more than the waist measure, as this length makes the front and back band. The pattern for children's drawers is so made that the front and back of the body may be either of equal or unequal length.

A scale of measurement for drawers of different sizes is here given, and the following diagram is drawn from a 22 hip to knee measure. The oblong is made 3 in. longer than this measure, to allow at the upper part of the pattern a slope of 3 in. from the folded edge to the back and front, if front and back are made the same length. The length of the seat usually determines the width of the oblong, and the judgment of the teacher is here exercised when the size of the pupil must be considered, as the oblong can be made wider or narrower.*

---

* A blackboard ruled into inch squares with red lines, every ninth line of some other color, to show the quarters of the yard, is a great help in the teaching and learning the proportions of diagrams.

Sectional paper ¼ in. scale is an aid to accurate and rapid work; every point and line may be drawn readily at the teacher's direction. It is also useful in reducing and drawing patterns.

These lessons on diagrams should be thoroughly learned before the drawing of them is attempted.

MEASUREMENT EXPRESSED IN INCHES FOR DIFFERENT SIZES OF DRAWERS.

Measurement from Upper Part of Hip to 3 in. below the Knee.	Lower end of Upper Slope.	Width of Upper Front Slope.	Width of Upper Back Slope.	Short Front Length, if desired.	Length of Seat.	Width from Folded Edge to Length of Seat is the width of the oblong.	Hem.	Edge for first turning of Hem.	Fold for Hem when turned for Sewing.
18	3	8	10	2	14	14	1¼	9¼	9
20	3	8	10	2	14	14	1¼	9¼	9
22	3	10	12	2	15	15	1½	9½	9
24	3	13	15	2	16	16	1½	10½	10
27	3	13	15	2½	18	18	1½	10½	10
30	4	13	15	2½	18	18	1½	12½	12

VII.

Pattern of drawers for a child of ten to twelve years (Fig. 68): —

This pattern consists of three pieces, — one-half of the drawers, and the front (Fig. 67, A) and back (Fig. 67, B) band. These bands are cut lengthwise of the cloth and sewed to the garment in the manner described in answer to question 65 in the second year. Make three buttonholes in each band. 1⅝ yds. of cloth 36 in. wide is needed for drawers of this size.

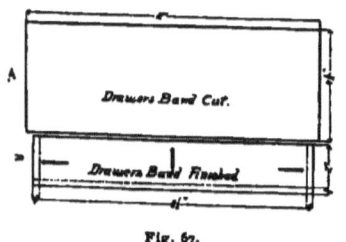

Fig. 67.

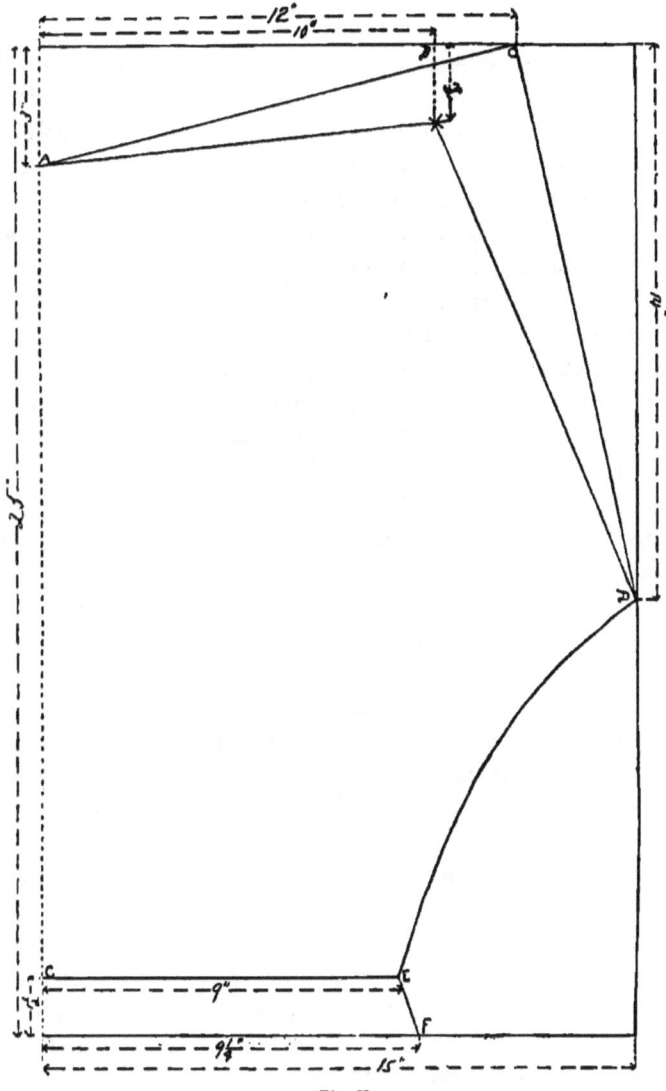

Fig. 68.

1. Draw upon the blackboard an oblong 15 in. × 25 in., with the shorter sides horizontal, making the left vertical a dotted line, to represent the line at which the cloth or paper is doubled.
2. From the upper left-hand corner of the oblong, measure 3 in. down on the dotted line, and mark the point A, for the lower end of the upper slope. From the upper end of the left vertical, measure to the right 10 in. Mark the point B, for the width of the upper front slope. From the same end measure to the right 12 in. Mark the point C, for the width of the upper back slope. Connect A–C by a straight line for the back slope.
3. From point B draw downward a dotted vertical line of 2 in., mark this point X. Connect A–X by a straight line for a short front length, if desired.
4. From the upper end on the right vertical, measure down 14 in. Mark the point D, for length of seat. Connect C–D for the back slope. Connect X–D for the front slope.
5. From the lower end of the left vertical line, measure upward 1½ in. Mark the point G, for width of the hem. From that point draw to the right a dotted horizontal line of 9 in. Mark the point E, for the fold of the hem. Connect D–E by curving gradually to the left. This gives the curve for the leg.
6. From the left end of the lower horizontal, measure to the right 9¼ in. Mark the point F. This leaves on the seam a slope for the hem. Connect E–F. Draw the pattern on paper.

Cut from A to C, C to D, to E, to F; and cut from A to X and X to D.

To make the opening at the side, from A cut down the fold 8 in. from the top. For binding, take a strip 17 in. long, selvedge way of the cloth, and bind the opening. Baste the binding on both sides of the opening, to the right side of the garment, by ¼ in. basting stitches.

Back-stitch close below the basting, then turn the strip over and hem to the wrong side directly over the stitching. This makes a very strong finish for the side, which will seldom wear or tear. Back-stitch and fell the seams.

For children it is more economical and quite as comfortable to leave the front and the back of the drawers of the same length; then, being worn evenly, the garment lasts longer.

Pattern for a chemise waist, for a child eight to ten years: —

This pattern consists of four pieces, one-half of the front and back, two pieces for the bias bands.

1⅔ yds. of yard-wide cloth are needed for two waists. One-half of this will not cut one waist.

FRONT (Fig. 69).

1. For the front draw an oblong 13 in. × 20 in., with the short sides horizontal, making the left vertical dotted to represent the line at which the cloth or paper is doubled.
2. From the upper left corner measure vertically downward on the dotted line 5¼ in. × 11 in. × 13½ in. Mark the points, respectively, A for the lower part of the front neck, K' for the upper, and R' for the lower edge of the bias band.
3. From the upper left corner measure horizontally to the right 3¼ in., marking the point B, for the upper part of the neck; 6¼ in., marking the point X, for length of shoulder; 9¼ in., marking the point Y, for width of arm-size. Connect B–A by a line, curving gradually to the right for the curve of the neck.
4. From the point X draw downward a dotted vertical 6½ in., and mark the lower end E, for length of arm-size. Mark the point C on this line 1 in. below the point X, for slope of shoulder seam. Connect the points B–C by a straight line to give the slope of the shoulder seam.

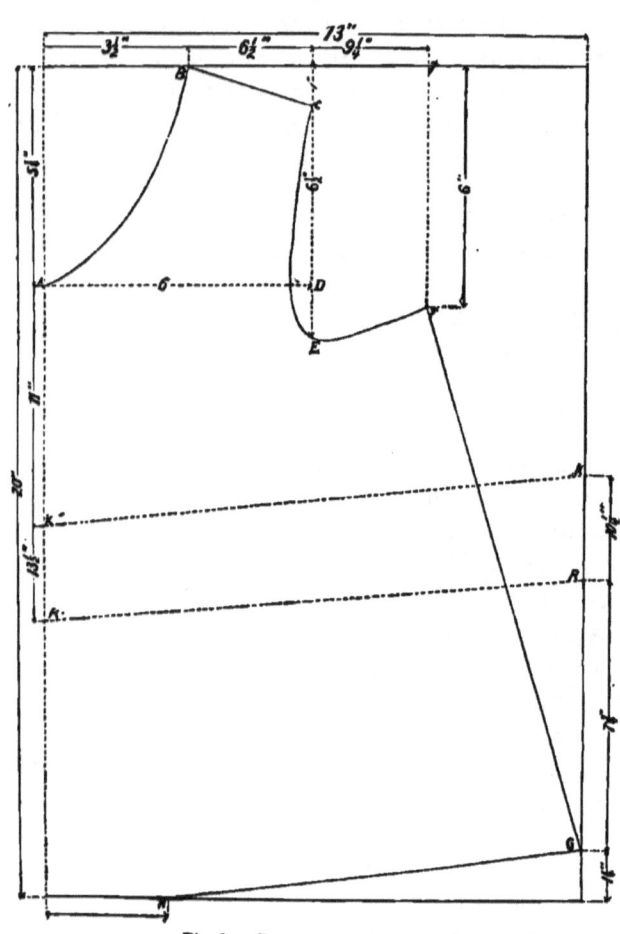

Fig. 59.—Front of chemise waist.

5. From Y draw downward a dotted vertical 6 in., and mark the point F, for the top of the under-arm seam.
6. From A draw a horizontal line 6 in. to the right, for width of chest, and mark the point D. Connect C, D, E, and F by a line curving to the left for the curve of the arm-size.
7. From the lower right corner measure vertically upward $1\frac{1}{4}$ in., and mark the point G; $7\frac{3}{4}$ in., and mark the point R; and $10\frac{1}{4}$ in., and mark the point K. Connect the points F and G by a straight line, to give the slope of the side seam. The points R–K are for the upper and lower edges of the bias band.
8. From the lower left corner measure 3 in. horizontally to the right, and mark the point H. Connect the points H and G, to give the slope at the lower end of the side seam.
9. Connect R and R' and K and K' by dotted lines, for the bias band at the waist.
10. Draw the pattern on paper and cut from A to B, C, D, E, F, G, and H.

This garment serves as a chemise and a waist, to which the drawers and skirts can be buttoned. It is a comfortable garment for children.

The band is made bias for elasticity and strength, and hemmed on the under side. It is $2\frac{1}{2}$ in. wide, to give opportunity to lower the buttons as the child grows.

BACK (Fig. 70).

1. For the back draw an oblong 11 in. × 19 in., the shorter sides horizontal, making the right vertical dotted, to represent the line at which the cloth or paper is doubled.

    From the upper left corner measure $1\frac{1}{2}$ in. horizontally to the right, and mark the point S. From this point draw a dotted vertical to the lower edge of the oblong, to mark the width of the hem at the back. On this line mark measurements for the lower part of back of neck and for width of bias band. From the upper end of

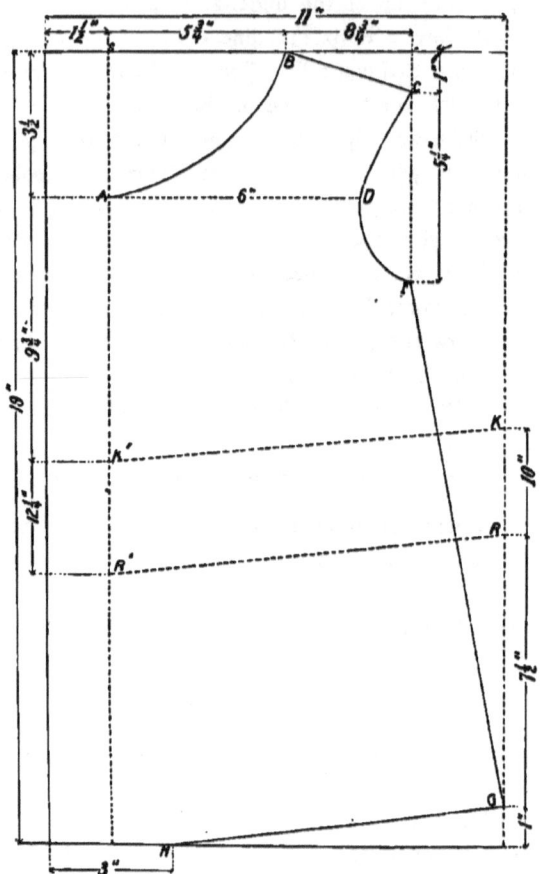

Fig. 70.—Back of chemise waist.

this line measure vertically downward 3½ in., 9¾ in., 12¼ in. Mark the points, respectively, A for the lower part of the back neck, K' for the upper, and R' for the lower edge of the bias band.
2. From the upper left corner of the oblong measure horizontally to the right 5¾ in., and mark the point B, for the upper part of the back neck; 8¾ in., mark X, for length of back shoulder. Connect A and B, to give the curve of the neck, by a line curving gradually to the right.
3. From A on the hem line make a dotted horizontal line 6 in. to the right, and mark the end D, for the width of the back.
4. From the point X draw downward a dotted vertical 5¼ in., and mark the lower end F, for the length of the back arm-size. Mark the point C on this line 1 in. below X. Connect B and C by a straight line, to give the slope for the shoulder seam. Connect C, D, and F by a line curving to the left, to give the curve of the back arm-size.
5. From the lower right corner measure up 1½ in., and mark the point G; 7½ in., mark the point R; and 10 in., and mark the point K. Connect F and G, to give the slope of the side seam. The points R and K are for the upper and lower edges of the bias band.
6. From the lower left corner of the oblong measure 3 in. to the right, mark the point H. Connect G and H by a straight line, to give the slope at the lower end of the side seam.
7. Connect R and R' and K and K' by straight lines for the bias band of the waist.
8. Draw the pattern on paper and fold over the hem at the hem line, then cut from A to B, C, D, E, F, and G.

Face the neck, arm-size, and lower edge with a strip of cloth cut on the bias.

The advantage of material cut on the bias is in its power to stretch when used as a facing on curves; and on a straight edge it makes a smoother lining than a straight strip of cloth. When cutting twilled fabric, fold the corner so that the lines of the twill will be perpendicular to the fold, crease firmly, and cut in the crease.

Cutting bias strips: —

Fold the bias edge the desired width, crease as before, cut in the

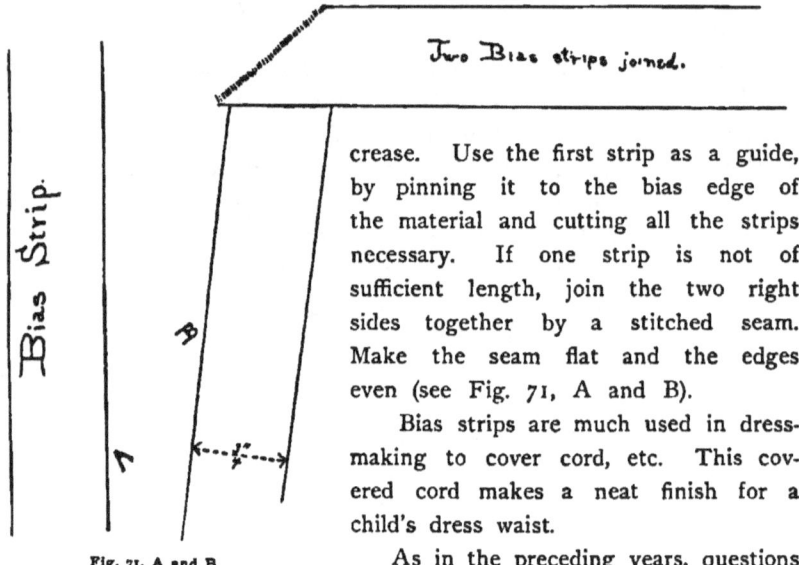

Fig. 71, A and B.

crease. Use the first strip as a guide, by pinning it to the bias edge of the material and cutting all the strips necessary. If one strip is not of sufficient length, join the two right sides together by a stitched seam. Make the seam flat and the edges even (see Fig. 71, A and B).

Bias strips are much used in dressmaking to cover cord, etc. This covered cord makes a neat finish for a child's dress waist.

As in the preceding years, questions on the work of the year are given out to the pupils from time to time, to which they are required to write full answers; but it is not thought necessary to specify these questions as heretofore.

CHAPTER V.

Fifth Year's Sewing.

FROM the paper patterns cut in the fourth year the pupils may now cut and make undergarments of fine white cotton. Flannel skirts are cut and made, either lengthwise or widthwise of the flannel; the seams are finished with herringbone or feather stitching; the hem is embroidered, if the pupil desires it. Diagrams are drawn for long tiers and for sleeves. The model form is studied (illustration of model form, Fig. 72).

If very good and careful work has been done in plain sewing, the pupil may select from their drawing lessons a design to arrange for embroidery or advanced Mexican work, and when the stitches have been thoroughly learned, a large part of this work can be done at home, thus leaving the study hours for that part of the work which must be done under the supervision of the teacher.

Study of the model form compared with the pupil's form:—

Study the general character of the model form and describe it.

The front is curved, the back is flat, the sides curve in slightly from the arm-size to the waist line, then curve outward.

Look at the cloth cover on the form; into how many parts is it divided? Tell the name of each part. Front, under-arm piece, back, side form for the back. These parts are joined together by seams.

Tell the names of these seams.

Dart or bias seams, under-arm seams (all seams from the last dart to the side-form seams are called under-arm seams), side-form seam (this is a curved seam and joined to the back), back centre seam, and shoulder seam. The fronts are joined or closed by a hem, but when the waist is opened at the back, a hem closes the back.

Notice the length of those parts which extend from the neck to the lower part of the waist; look at the shorter parts; notice and describe the dart seams.

The use of a dart or bias is to lessen the fulness of the cloth and make the part smaller.

Measure around the lower part of the waist for a belt. Make a belt 1½ in. wide and 2 in. longer than the waist measure, so that one end of the belt can lie over the other end for a lap. Pin this belt close around the smallest part of the waist, that all vertical measurements may be made from its lowest edge, that edge being called the waist line.

Fig. 72.—Model form.

MEASURING THE FORM.

1. From the lower part of the neck curve, measure vertically to the waist line; this makes a front centre line.
2. Measure from the lower edge of the front centre of the belt to the upper edge of the shoulder seam on the neck. Make a note of this and all following measurements.
3. Measure horizontally from the lower part of the shoulder to the front centre line. Observe the distance from the centre line to the first dart seam and to the second dart seam. Measure hori-

zontally the distance from the top of the darts to this centre line, also from these darts at the waist line to the centre line. Compare these measures; tell how they differ; notice that the cloth has been drawn into a small space to make this difference. Measure horizontally from the top of the last dart to the first under-arm seam; to the second under-arm seam. At the waist line, from the last dart, measure to these under-arm seams. Compare these measurements; tell how they differ. From the waist line at the centre of the back measure vertically to the centre of the back neck. Measure horizontally from the lower edge of the shoulder seam to this back centre seam; from the lower part of the back arm-size, measure horizontally to this back centre seam. Notice where the side form joins the back by a curved seam, and where this curved seam begins at the back arm-size. At the waist line, measure the distance from the back centre seam to this curved seam; measure from this curved seam to the second under-arm seam at the waist line. On the blackboard make a diagram of these parts. Make diagrams on paper, cut them out, pin them to the form, and see how they compare with the parts of the cover.

When a pupil has gained a knowledge of the form, let her take a sheet of thin manilla paper and make a pattern of the cloth cover by pinning the paper to the form and using its seams as a guide for the seams in her paper pattern. Then make a pattern in cloth. When a satisfactory pattern has been made in cloth, let the pupil tell in writing how she made it. Take measurements like these on the pupil's form and cut a paper pattern from them. Let a teacher not be discouraged when her pupil fails to make a perfect pattern from these measurements, since this is but preparatory work, and pupils have not yet sufficient judgment necessary for perfect work.

PATTERN FOR A TIER.

This pattern consists of five pieces: one-half of the front, one-half of the back, upper and under part of sleeve, and neck band.

PATTERN OF THE FRONT OF TIER, HAVING CHEST MEASURE OF 29 IN. AND LENGTH MEASURE OF 40 IN. (Fig. 73).

Measurements: —

For the length of the tier, measure from the upper part of the shoulder to the lower edge of the dress skirt. For the chest measure, pass the tape over the chest, under the arms, and across the back. Allow the tape measure to lie smoothly over these parts and observe the number of inches.

1. Draw upon the blackboard an oblong 18 in. × 40 in., the shorter sides horizontal; and make the left vertical dotted, to represent the line where the cloth or paper is doubled.
2. From the upper left corner, measure vertically down $4\frac{1}{2}$ in. and mark the point A, for the lower part of the front neck. From the point A, draw to the right a horizontal dotted line $7\frac{1}{4}$ in. and mark the right end D, for width of chest.
3. From the upper left corner, measure horizontally to the right $2\frac{1}{2}$ in. for the upper part of the front neck, 8 in. and 10 in. for the length of shoulder and width of arm-size, marking the points respectively B, X, and Y. Connect B and A by a line curving gradually to the right, for the curve of the neck.
4. From the point X draw downward a dotted vertical of 8 in. and mark the lower end E, for length of arm-size. On this line mark the point C 1 in. below X. Connect C and B by a straight line for the slope of the shoulder.
5. From Y draw downward a dotted vertical $7\frac{1}{2}$ in. and mark the lower end F, for the upper end of the under-arm seam. Beginning at C, connect C, D, E, and F by a line which curves gradually to the left, for the arm-size.

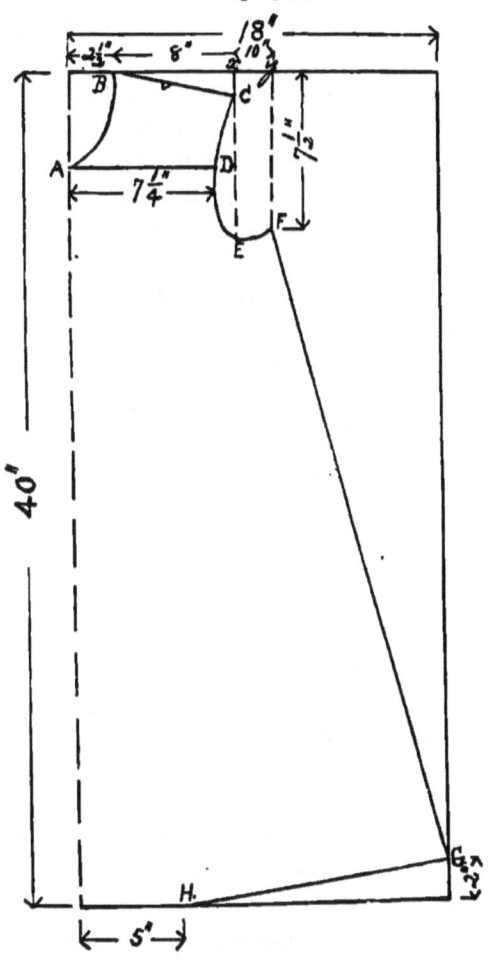

Scale $\tfrac{1}{8}" = 1"$

Fig. 73.

6. From the lower right corner, measure upward 2 in. on the right vertical and mark the point G. Connect F and G by a straight line for the side seam.
7. From the lower left corner, measure horizontally to the right 5 in. and mark the point H. Connect G and H by a straight line, to give the slope at the lower end of the side seam.
8. Copy on doubled paper and cut from A to B, C, D, E, F, G, and H, leaving $\frac{1}{2}$ in. outside the shoulders and side lines for seams.

PATTERN OF THE BACK OF TIER (Fig. 74).

1. Draw upon the blackboard an oblong 18 in. × 39 in., the short sides horizontal, and the left vertical dotted, to represent the line where the cloth or paper is doubled.
2. From the upper right corner, measure horizontally to the left 2 in.; mark this point A. From A draw a vertical line to the lower edge of the oblong. This line gives the width of the hem for buttons and buttonholes at the back.
3. From the upper right corner, measure horizontally to the left 4 in., $9\frac{1}{2}$ in., and $10\frac{1}{2}$ in., for the length of the shoulder seams, marking the points respectively B, X, and Y.
4. From X draw downward a dotted vertical line 4 in. and mark the lower end D, for the curve of the back arm-size. On this line mark the point C, $1\frac{1}{2}$ in. below X, for lower end of shoulder seam. Connect B and C by a straight line.
5. From the point Y draw downward a dotted vertical $6\frac{1}{2}$ in. and mark the lower end F. Connect C, D, and F for the curve of the arm-size by a line which curves slightly to the right.
6. From the lower left corner, measure upward 2 in. on the left vertical and mark the point G. Connect F and G by a straight line for the side seam.

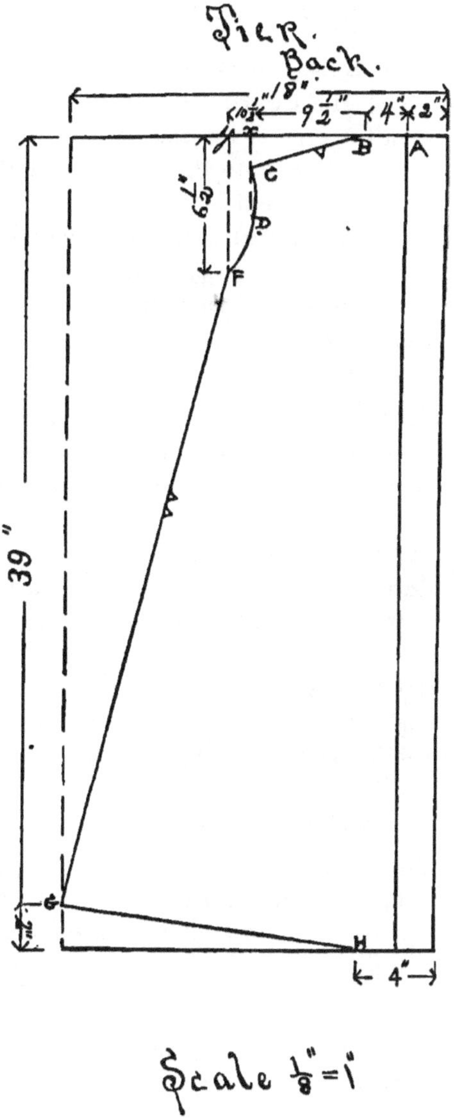

Scale $\frac{1}{8}"=1$

Fig. 74.

7. From the lower right corner, measure horizontally to the left 4 in. and mark the point H. Connect G and H by a straight line, for the slope at the lower edge of the side seam.
8. Copy on paper and cut from A to B, C, D, E, and F, leaving $\frac{1}{2}$ in. outside the shoulder and side lines for seams.
9. Cut the cloth from the paper pattern thus made. For this tier it requires 3 yds. of cloth from 26 in. to 30 in. wide, according to the size of the child. The pattern will fit pupils from ten to thirteen or fourteen years of age. When 26 in. material is used, small gores may be placed at the lower end of the side seam to make the required width.

The back of the tier is made shorter than the front, that the shoulder seam may be sewed 1 in. below the top of the shoulder. The front is carried over the shoulder to meet this line, and for this reason is made 1 in. longer.

Baste with $\frac{1}{4}$ in. stitches, $\frac{1}{8}$ in. spaces, and sew together the seams that are notched alike. Measure the number of inches around the neck of the tier, and make a band from the selvedge way of the cloth $2\frac{1}{2}$ in. wide and $\frac{1}{2}$ in. longer than the size of the neck. Baste the band to the neck (laying the right sides together), then stitch the tier to the band, fold over $\frac{1}{8}$ in. of the raw edges on the side and ends; oversew the ends, and hem down the side. Make the buttonholes on the right hem, and sew the buttons on the left hem.

SLEEVE PATTERN FOR TIER.

This pattern consists of two pieces; they are called upper and under parts of the sleeve. The upper part is much larger than the under part, that the two seams (the inner seam and the outer seam) may not be easily seen when the sleeve is worn.

Measuring for a sleeve: —

Begin 2 in. above the shoulder joint, carry the tape measure to the bended elbow, and note the distance from the shoulder joint to this point; continue with the tape measure to the wrist and note the distance from the elbow to the wrist. Measure from the upper end of the first under-arm seam of the dress to the wrist; notice the measure at the bend of the arm. When sewing the sleeve to the garment, the sleeve should be held next the sewer.

FRONT OR UPPER PART OF THE SLEEVE (Fig. 75).

To draw a diagram for sleeve, when the arm on the outside measures 14 in. from shoulder joint to bended elbow; 10 in. from bended elbow to wrist; 8 in. from upper part of under-arm seam to elbow; 8 in. from elbow to wrist.

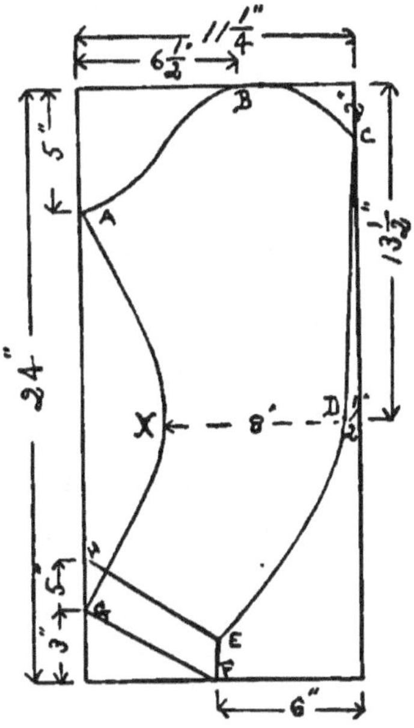

1. Draw an oblong 11 in. × 24 in., the short sides horizontal.
2. From the upper left corner, measure down 5 in. on the left vertical and mark the point A. From the same corner, measure horizontally to the right 6½ in. and mark the point B. Connect A and B by a reversed curve, that curves slightly to the right and then slightly to the left, to give the curve to the top of the sleeve.
3. From the upper right-hand corner, measure down on the right vertical 2 in. and mark the point C. Connect B and C by a line that curves slightly to the right; this completes the top line of the sleeve.
4. From the upper right corner, measure down on the right vertical

Fig. 75.

13½ in. and mark the elbow point D, ½ in. in from the right vertical. Connect C and D by a straight line for the upper part of the back seam.

5. From the lower right corner, measure horizontally to the left 6 in. and mark the point F. From F measure vertically upward 1½ in. and mark this point E. Connect E and F by a straight line for the back slope of the hem of the lower part of the sleeve. Connect E with D by a line which curves slightly to the right; this finishes the lower part of the back seam.

6. From the lower left corner, measure up on the left vertical 3 in. and 5 in. and mark the points respectively G and H. Connect G and F by a straight line for the lower edge of the sleeve. Connect H and E by a straight line for the line at which the hem is folded.

7. From D draw to the left a dotted horizontal of 8 in. (less or more according to the width desired at the elbow) and mark the left end X. Connect A, X, and G by a line which curves gradually to the right. This line gives the curve for the inner or front seam of the sleeve. Copy upon paper and cut from A to B, C, D, E, F, G, H, X, and A.

BACK OR UNDER PART OF SLEEVE (Fig. 76).

1. Draw on the blackboard an oblong 8½ in. × 22 in., with the shorter sides horizontal.
2. From the upper left corner, measure horizontally to the right 2¼ in. and 7 in. and mark the points respectively C and X. From X draw downward a dotted vertical 3½ in. and mark the lower end A. Connect C and A by a line which curves downward and which reaches its lowest point quite near A, making a curve on the top of the under part of the sleeve.
3. From the upper left corner, measure down on the left vertical

12½ in. and mark the elbow point D. Connect C and D by a straight line for the upper part of the back seam.

4. From the lower left corner, measure horizontally to the right 4½ in. and mark the point F. From the point F measure vertically upward 1½ in. and mark the point E. Connect E and F by a straight line for the back slope of the hem at the lower part of the sleeve. Connect D and E by a line two-thirds of which is straight, one-third curved. The curve begins 3 in. below D and continues to D for the elbow curve. This finishes the lower part of the back seam.

5. From the lower right corner, measure up on the right vertical 2½ in. and 4 in., marking the points respectively G and H. Connect F and G by a straight line for the lower edge of the sleeve. Connect E and H by a straight line for the line upon which the hem is to be folded.

6. From D draw to the right a dotted horizontal of 5 in. (less or more according to the width desired at the elbow) and mark the right end X. Connect A, X, and G by a line which curves gradually to the left and becomes straight from X to G. This line gives the curve for the inner or front seam of the sleeve. Copy upon paper and cut from C to D, E, F, G, X, and A to C.

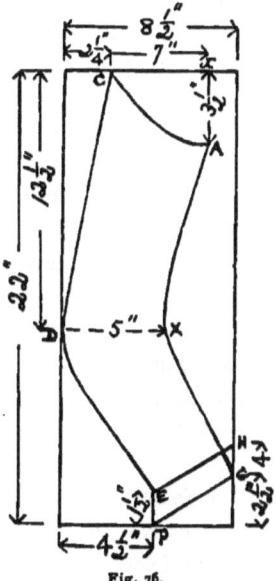

Fig. 76.

After a pupil has drawn the sleeve on paper and cut by the lines, she can compare the parts until familiar with all the lines and can see how these two parts differ and how they must be placed to fit the arm. The cloth may next be cut from the paper pattern.

BASTING AND MAKING A SLEEVE.

When the cloth has been cut from this pattern, place the lower edges of the inner seam evenly together and baste from this point to the top; place the lower edges of the back seam evenly together and baste in the same way. Stitch the seam below the basting; turn, baste, and sew the hem. At the top of the upper part of the sleeve make two lines of running stitches, the first line $\frac{1}{4}$ in., the second $\frac{1}{2}$ in. below the top edge, with which to gather the fulness. Make a notch in the edge at the point B, and place this point 1 in. in front of the shoulder seam on the arm-size, and then arrange the fulness to the arm-size 4 in. in front of B and 2 in. back of B, being careful to keep the inner seam of the sleeve well under the arm. This pattern allows for one-half inch seams.

When a coat sleeve with a full top is desired for the sleeve of a dress, cut by this tier sleeve pattern; if it is too loose below the arm-size, curve the back seam to fit the arm.

In cutting sleeves, never double the cloth except in double width material, because the four pieces can be cut more economically from single cloth.

Pupils should learn to cut some of their patterns freehand.

The following description is for a blouse or shirt sleeve. The pupil watches the teacher, who cuts out the pattern from a doubled piece of paper, the folded edge of which is used as an inner seam. After the upper side of the sleeve is cut, the paper is unfolded, and the curve of the top is cut for the under side. The pattern is then tried on the arm and pared to fit exactly. The pupil now takes the pattern and traces it upon the blackboard. She then spreads the pattern upon her desk and compares it carefully with the one drawn on the blackboard. She then erases the drawing on the blackboard and draws on paper, freehand, a sleeve for the right arm, then a sleeve for the left arm. She then takes a piece of paper and cuts freehand this pattern of a sleeve.

ORNAMENT.

In this year a pleasing arrangement can be made from their drawing lessons (Fig. 77) for a design to embroider in couching, French knot, and outline-stitch, not alone for ornament, but to lead the pupil to

Fig. 77.—Design for embroidery from a drawing lesson.

study the grace and beauty of designs for that kind of needlework which will make a garment or any article to which it is applied more beautiful, thus carrying into ornament what has been learned for actual use, such as hemstitching, darning, herringbone stitch, etc.

Embroidery darning is for ornament and is worked on the right side of the cloth. It is made with straight edges and without loops.

The stitch is the same as that used in darning a thin place which is not yet worn into holes.

Couching is fastening a cord on a piece of work by oversewing or by embroidery edging stitches; it is used only in ornamental work (Fig. 78).

To make a French knot, fasten the thread with a rolled knot on the under side; then bring the needle to the upper side, pulling the thread through the cloth. Hold it by the left thumb down to the cloth at nearly an inch from this place, and pass the needle alternately under and over the thread from above to below between this place and the thumb, pointing it toward the thumb. Turn the needle back and pass it perpendicularly through to the under side as near as possible to the place where the thread comes up, then draw the thread through, not too tight.

Fig. 78.—Couching.

With heavy worsted there should be but one twist, with silk or cotton two or more twists about the needle, according to the size of the knot required. This French knot is used only for embroidery.

Outline-stitch is the stitch with which designs are outlined, and is also used to fill in on some kinds of embroidery.

To make outline stitch, the work should be held so that the line to be embroidered runs from the person. Fasten the thread by three running stitches along this line; with the needle pointing toward the chest, draw the thread through until but two stitches remain in the cloth; this leaves the end on the under side. Now carry the needle $\frac{1}{8}$ in. backward over these stitches, and take up on it four threads along the line of the design with the needle still pointing toward the chest, and the loop of the thread held to the right of the line. Draw the needle through, and carry it backward another $\frac{1}{8}$ in. along the line of the design, and continue as before; and so on. At points or corners the ingenuity of the worker must be exercised in deciding how to shorten the stitch, and where to put the needle through so as to preserve the outline.

When a large design is made, or worked on coarse material, a longer stitch is made.

CHAPTER VI.

Sixth Year's Sewing.

The training of previous years should have taught pupils the best way of preparing and finishing work, so that the time in this year may be used in gaining a practical knowledge of cutting, fitting, and making simple cotton dresses.

Linings for these dresses are fitted by the pupils to some girl's form; this work together with the practice in measuring makes a thorough foundation for the future study of a "System for Dress-cutting." That process of fitting is more rapid when the proportions of a form are well understood. A gored skirt is often used for a skirt lining or for an under-skirt, and a pattern for this is made from measurement this year.

In connection with this instruction, talks are to be given on what constitutes true and refined taste in dress. The pupil should learn that a good material simply made is always appropriate, attractive, and serviceable. The talks on good taste are illustrated and enforced when buying neat prints and ginghams for school practice, and by showing how to make garments fit well.

The importance of considering individual form in the choice of material, and in the pattern and style of dress, should be pointed out. For instance, fulness in waist or skirt, which is becoming to a slender person, is very unbecoming to a stout person, especially if she is short also. A tall and slender person, to whom checks are becoming, should avoid stripes that run lengthwise, as they apparently add to her height. A short person looks shorter and broader in plaids or large checks. Flounces decrease the appearance of height and add to the width, as do tucks and puffings. Narrow lengthwise pleats seemingly add to the height. Plain, dark colored cloths make the figure appear slighter than do light colored cloths. These and similar facts should be considered before a dress is bought.

Also that the number of yards of material needed for a dress depends upon the size of the person to be fitted and the width of the material to be used.

The teacher may have for this class a book of fashion plates, such as would be appropriate for pupils to use when choosing designs for making their own dresses; and also a few patterns to assist them in forming others; this practice will lay the foundation for dress designing. Crayons or water colors can be used advantageously to illustrate patterns.

Especial care should be taken with the basting, as a waist which is well cut may be spoiled by careless basting. The waist seams should have bastings $\frac{1}{8}$ in. long, like the first basting taught on canvas.

In basting wide hems and facings, several points should be carefully observed: —

1. Any large piece of work, like a dress skirt, should be laid upon a table or desk, the doubled edge of the hem nearest the worker. Then the work is not being dragged out of the hands by its own weight.

2. The hem to be basted should lie flat upon the table, while the fingers of the left hand move along the hem in front of the needle, as it is pushed through by the right hand; this holds the hem in place. The basting should be kept evenly $\frac{1}{8}$ in. from the folded edge of the hem. This practice greatly helps a person to properly baste linings to the dress material, although the basting stitches are there made longer, and one inch from the cut edges.

3. When turning the hem in checked or striped cloths, care should be taken to match the checks or stripes at each seam. If they are exactly

matched on the hem, there will be no further trouble with them. *Good results depend on careful preparation.*

Great care should be used in cutting plaids: they are very difficult to match, and material is often wasted when not cut by the right line. When the checks are of two colors, say pink and white, cut them so as to separate the checks exactly, then the whole pink checks will be on one end of the length, and the whole white checks on the other end. Join the pink checks for the lower edge of the skirt, and all the white checks will be on the upper edge of the lengths. Uneven plaids, if cut exactly in the centre of the checks or close to the edge of the check, can be matched the same way.

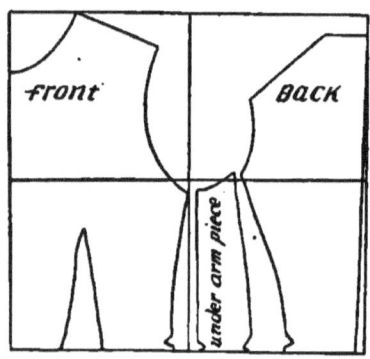

Fig. 79.—Pattern of a round waist.

When a pupil has obtained good results in cutting and fitting a round waist pattern from paper and cambric, then cloth for a dress lining can be given to her. After cutting a round waist lining, she can be taught the difference between a round waist and a basque.

A round waist is often made with one dart at each side of the front and has all its seams finished at the waist line (Fig. 79). A basque differs from it in having all the seams fitted below the waist line; two or more darts at each side of the front; one or more under-arm pieces for each side of the waist; and one side form for each side of the back (Fig. 80). The back of a basque, like the round waist, is divided by a centre seam. The centre pieces of the back have a gradual curve from the back arm-size to the waist line. Particular attention should be given to these back centre parts, as the symmetry of the entire back depends on their proportion. For a 24 in. waist these centre pieces should measure at the waist line 1½ in. after the seams are sewed; they should be increased or lessened according to the size of the waist.

To fit a basque lining: —

For a form which has a bust measure of 32 in. and waist measure of 24 in., take 1¼ yds. of lining. (The cut edges are on the width of

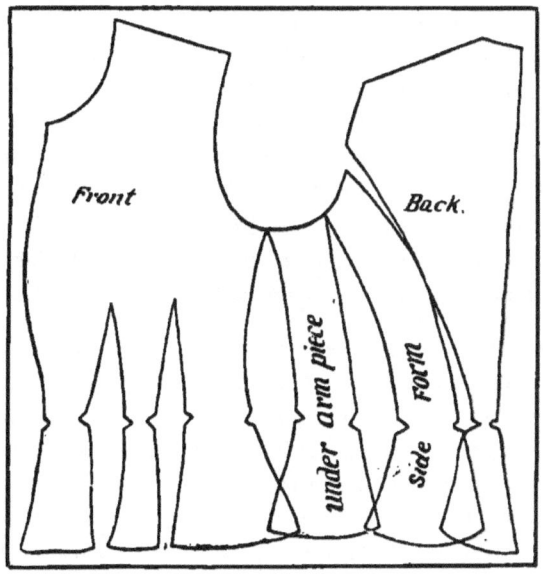

Fig. 80 — Pattern of a basque.

the cloth.) Pin the cut edges together, as the cloth is to be cut double, and both sides of the lining are fitted to one side of the form. Turn 1½ in. for a hem. The width is now vertical, the length of the cloth horizontal. The width threads of cloth stretch in wearing, and the lining is cut in this way to remove all tendency to wear short-waisted.

To pin the lining to the model form:—

From one end of the fold of the hem, measure vertically $4\frac{1}{2}$ in. From the same end, measure horizontally 2 in. Cut the curve from $4\frac{1}{2}$ in. to 2 in., place the $4\frac{1}{2}$ in. point at the lower part of the front neck and pin the hem to the centre of the front, placing the pins $1\frac{1}{2}$ in. apart. Pin down the desired length for a basque.

To form the darts:—

From the folded edges of the hem at the fullest part of the chest, measure horizontally to the left 3 in. and $5\frac{1}{2}$ in., place a pin at the 3 in. point and at $5\frac{1}{2}$ in. point, for the top of the darts. Pin the darts in the same manner as in the round waist, fitting the seams below the waist line. The darts will now be $2\frac{1}{2}$ in. apart at the top, 1 in. apart at the waist line, and $1\frac{1}{2}$ in. at the lower edge of the basque. Draw the lining smoothly and pin it to the shoulder. From the folded edges of the hem smooth and pin the lining to the arm-size and under the arm; cut the arm-size.

To fit the under-arm pieces:—

Pin vertically two straight pieces of the lining together (to hold the under pieces together while fitting); pin these pieces by a horizontal thread to the waist line, and pin by a vertical thread from the waist line to the arm-size; continue the front curve of the arm-size by cutting these pieces; pin the fronts to the under-arm pieces, making the curve for the body on the fronts and below the waist line. This makes the first under-arm seam.

To fit the back:—

Using the cloth double, fold $1\frac{1}{2}$ in. as for a hem, pin this fold down the centre of the back, placing the pins $1\frac{1}{2}$ in. apart. Five in. above the waist line, pin a dart beginning with one thread (as in a front dart), curve this dart to the form, making it $\frac{1}{4}$ in. wide at the waist line; then curve outward below the waist line to fit the form. Beginning at the neck, smooth the lining from the pinned fold to the shoulder, pin the front and back together for the shoulder seam, which should be 5 in. long. Make this seam 1 in. back from the top of the shoulder.

To cut the back arm-size and curve for the side form: —

Cut vertically downward 3 in. from the lower end of the shoulder seam for the back arm-size; from this point cut the curve for the side form, making the back centre pieces 2 in. wide at the waist line.

To fit the side form: —

Pin two straight pieces of the lining by a horizontal thread to the waist line and pin by a vertical thread from the waist line to the upper part of the curve; pin this side form smoothly to the curve, taking $\frac{1}{4}$ in. seam from the back curve; this seam curves the side form exactly like the back; below the waist line the side form has a straight edge. (We are describing a plain basque, — all these seams can be altered at the fancy of the maker.) The curve to fit the body below the waist line is cut on the front edge of the back centre pieces. Pin the side forms to the under-arm piece. Having brought the front and back smoothly together, begin pinning these parts together half-way between the waist line and the arm-size; from this point continue pinning the seam down to the waist line, then pin from the centre of the seam to the arm-size. By following these directions, the seam will not wrinkle. The curve to fit the body below the waist line is cut on the back edge of the under-arm piece. When all the seams are securely pinned, take the pins from the front hem and from the back centre fold, pare all the seams to within 1 in. of the pins. Make a notch in every seam at the waist line for guides to commence basting the different parts together. A dress waist, to be in good proportion, should have that part of the waist lining which is between the last dart and first under-arm seam nearly equal in measurement to the back side form and under-arm piece (or pieces).

If the eye is trained in proportions, a good pattern may be cut without exact measurement.

A round waist or a basque lining may be fitted to a pupil's form in the same manner. Before fitting to the form, let a pupil draw on the blackboard a picture of a round waist like Fig. 79; then, on a pupil's form, measure from the top of the neck curve to the waist line; take her chest measure according to direction for the tier; make an oblong from these measurements, using the first measure for the length, and one-half of the second measure for the width of the oblong; divide this oblong into four parts by connecting the middle points of the opposite sides. In this oblong draw freehand a picture of a round waist, using the dividing lines as guides for its proportions. This practice is a great help in learning proportions.

Thin white cotton is best for lining a wash dress, because it has no color to stain the dress when it is laundered. This lining should be laundered before cutting, then the shrinking will not affect the fitting. For a girl fourteen years old, 1 yd. of lining is needed for a round waist, and $1\frac{1}{4}$ yds. of lining for a basque.

Choose from the book of models the pattern from which to make a dress. Make a picture of this on the blackboard with colored crayons, and on drawing paper with pencil and colored inks (Fig. 81). Then cut from stiff manilla paper a waist and skirt lining, as if for a good-sized doll; baste these together and use them for a foundation over which striped or checked tissue paper can be pasted or sewed in the style chosen, being careful to match checks or stripes. This gives a model in miniature (see Fig. 82).

Fig. 81.—Pupil's drawing from a book of models.

Then take the thinnest kind of manilla paper to represent the dress material, and pin it over the dress lining in the same manner as the tissue paper was arranged on the small model. Use the manilla paper for a pattern from which to cut the dress material.

In cutting the dress goods, be careful to have the corresponding pieces for the two sides of the waist correct. If both are cut together, the cloth must be folded so that the right sides lie together. Single width cloth can be cut more economically if not folded. If one piece is cut first, it should be laid either right side on the right side, or wrong side on the wrong side, of the cloth from which the other is to be cut. Show on the blackboard the proper position of the right sleeve to the left sleeve when cut correctly. *Be very exact in cutting curves.*

After the dress material is cut, the pieces should be laid on the corresponding pieces of the lining, and the two smoothly basted together 1 in. from the edge, with stitches from 1 in. to $1\frac{1}{2}$ in. long. The seams should then be basted with short basting stitches of $\frac{1}{3}$ in., always beginning at the notches made at the waist line.

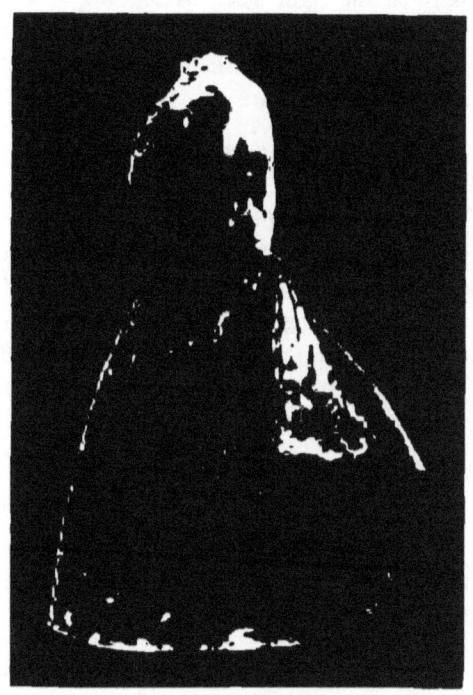

Fig. 82. — Paper dress made by a pupil.

To prepare a plain round skirt for sewing to the waist or band: —

Divide the skirt and waist or band into corresponding halves by cross-stitches of a colored thread, which show readily against the cloth. Turn the top edge until the skirt is the desired length. Gather the skirt on the right side, making the stitches $\frac{1}{2}$ in. long and spaces $\frac{1}{8}$ in. long for gathering the back breadth; gathering stitches $\frac{1}{4}$ in. long and spaces $\frac{1}{8}$ in. for the side breadths; for the front breadth even stitches and spaces of $\frac{1}{8}$ in.

To sew a skirt to the waist or band: —

Pin the centres of the waist and skirt firmly together; hold the skirt and gathers toward the sewer, take one gather on each stitch, and sew firmly with strong thread. Sew the gathers of the back breadth into a space $4\frac{1}{2}$ in. long. The gathers of the front breadth sew into a space 9 in. long. The side breadths should be sewed between these measures. If the figure requires more fulness at the sides than this gives, the gathers can be spread a little from the front and back. This description is for a skirt made from four widths of gingham.

PATTERN OF ONE-HALF OF GORED SKIRT (Fig. 83).

This pattern consists of three pieces, viz. front, back, and side gore, which is one-half the skirt. Quantity of material 24 in. wide needed for a skirt, 4 yds.

HALF OF FRONT BREADTH.

1. Draw on the blackboard an oblong 11 in. × 36 in., having the shorter lines horizontal and the left vertical a dotted line, to show where the cloth or paper is doubled.
2. From the left upper corner, measure horizontally to the right $2\frac{1}{2}$ in., $3\frac{1}{2}$ in., $7\frac{3}{4}$ in., and 9 in., marking the points respectively A, B, C, and D.

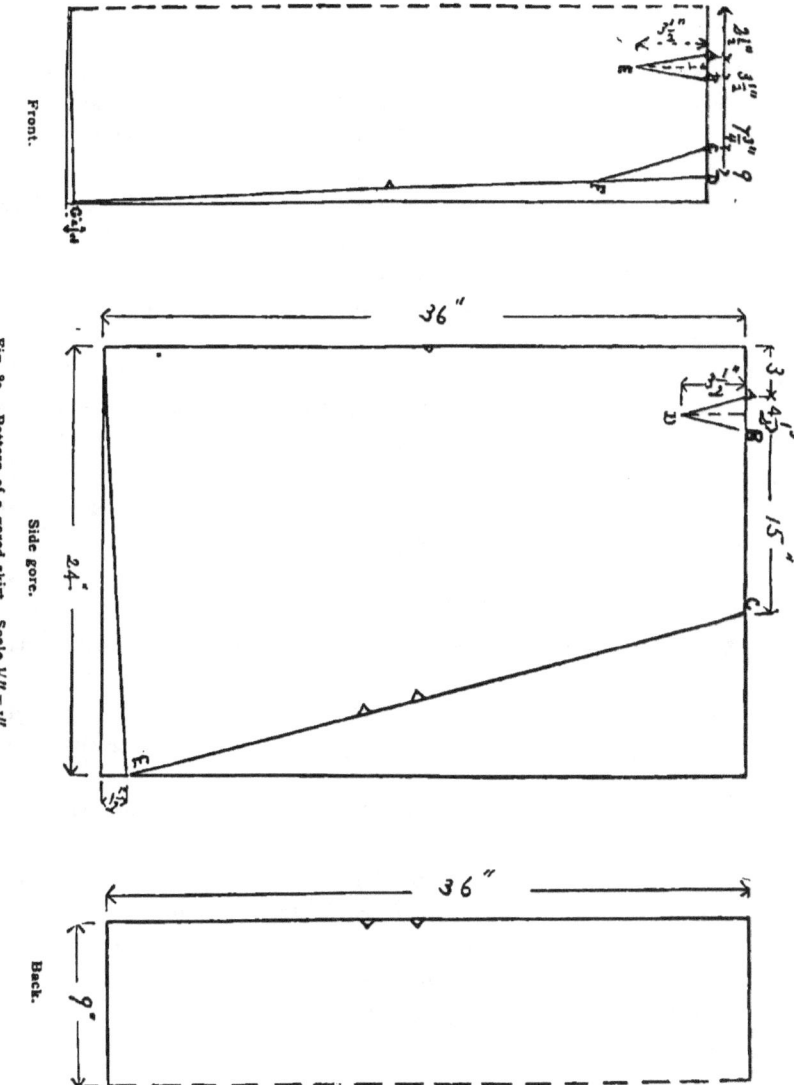

Fig. 83.—Pattern of a gored skirt. Scale ⅛″ = 1″.

3. Half-way between A and B draw downward a dotted vertical $3\frac{1}{2}$ in. long, and mark the lower end E. Connect points A, E, and B, E, by straight lines; this gives the V which is folded over or cut, to fit the skirt to the waist.
4. From the lower right corner, measure up on the right vertical $\frac{1}{2}$ in. and mark the point G. Connect the points D and G by a straight line for a seam. Mark one notch on the centre of this line, to show the edges which must be joined together in sewing.
5. On the line connecting D–G, mark the point F_1 6 in. below D, and connect C and F by a straight line for the slope on the hip.
6. Draw a straight line from the lower left corner to G; this line slopes the lower edge of the front breadth, making it even with the straight edge of the side gore.

SIDE GORE.

1. Draw on the blackboard an oblong 24 in. × 36 in., making the shorter lines horizontal.
2. From the upper left corner, measure horizontally to the right 3 in., $4\frac{1}{4}$ in., and 15 in., marking the points respectively A, B, and C.
3. Half-way between A and B draw downward a dotted vertical $3\frac{1}{2}$ in. long and mark the lower end D.
4. Connect the points A–D and B–D by straight lines; this gives the V by which the skirt is fitted to the waist in this gore.
5. From the lower right corner, measure up on the right vertical $1\frac{1}{2}$ in. and mark the point E. Connect E and C by a straight line for the slope of the side gore. In the centre of this line mark two notches, and one notch in the centre of the left vertical line.

6. From the lower left corner draw a straight line to the point E. This line slopes the lower edge of the side gore, making it even with the straight edge of the back breadth.

BACK BREADTH.

1. Draw on the blackboard an oblong 9 in. × 36 in., the shorter lines horizontal, and the right vertical dotted, to show where the cloth is doubled.
2. Mark two notches in the centre of the left vertical, to correspond with the notches in the side gore.

In putting the breadths together, several points must be carefully observed.

1. Baste together a straight and gored edge according as they are notched, — an edge having one notch to an edge having one notch, an edge having two notches to an edge having two notches.
2. Always hold the gored edge to the person in basting or sewing.
3. In order to keep the gored edges always toward the person in working, two seams on one side of the skirt should be commenced at the top, the top edges being exactly even; the seams opposite must be commenced at the bottom, and the lower edges can be measured and arranged from the side already done.

The even hanging of the skirt depends upon the careful observation of these points.

Cut evenly the lower edge of the skirt. Make all seams of equal length, turn the upper edge until the skirt is the desired length. Sew a bias facing 4 in. wide to the lower edge of the skirt, and gather (as a round skirt) the upper edge of the back breadth and the side gores to the V. Oversew to the band or waist, as a round skirt, being careful to fasten the gathering threads when the oversewing is finished.

4. From the middle of the top of the back breadth cut down 9 in. for a placket. The front breadth and part of the side gores are fitted to the band by basting the V to fit the figure.

APPENDIX.

The following papers, prepared by the pupils, are added to show the relation of drawing and language to needlework; demonstrating a lesson in this way makes the work educational as well as practical.

THIRD YEAR'S SEWING.

A Stitched-in Patch.

I first cut the worn or torn place out square. The four edges are made true by a drawn thread. Then I make the bias cuts, which are small cuts ¼ in. in each corner, and crease the edges to mark for a line of stitching. Then I mark the lengthwise of my cloth and patch by a pin or a crease. I lay the patch on the under side, and baste the edges even, first taking a few stitches out on the patch; and when one side is finished, I sew a few stitches out on the other side of patch, as before. This is to make the corners square. I then cut the thread, and turn to the width of my cloth, and begin out on the patch. Then I sew the sides, as I

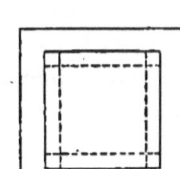
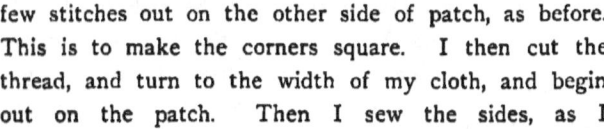
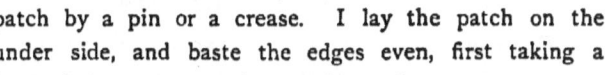

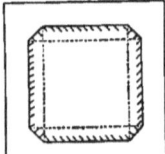 did before, until I have the four sides sewed, and overcast the raw edges.

My first diagram represents the torn or worn place.

My second diagram represents the torn or worn place cut out square; the dotted lines show where it is creased.

My third diagram represents the patch basted on to the garment.

My fourth diagram represents the patch stitched in, and the edges overcast.

My fifth diagram represents the patch finished.

MARY STEVERMAN

W. H. Lincoln School.   (Age 12 years).

SECOND YEAR'S SEWING.

For oversewing we put the two edges together, and baste $\frac{1}{16}$ in. from the top. We use No. 2. basting line. We begin at the right hand, and sew to the left.

We commence oversewing by taking a stitch on the right-hand end; draw the thread all but $\frac{1}{2}$ in., put that $\frac{1}{2}$ in. on the top, and go on 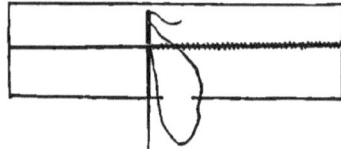 sewing over it three stitches. If the end of the thread is now seen, cut it off.

Joining.

To join a new thread, we go back three stitches, then take a stitch and pull the thread through, leaving $\frac{1}{2}$ in.; put that on the top with the other end; sew over it four stitches. If the end is seen, cut it off; when we are through, we sew back two stitches.

AGNES BROWN

W. H. Lincoln School.   (Age 10 years).

THIRD YEAR'S SEWING.
How I sew on a Wristband.

In preparing a piece of cloth to sew to a band, I find the middle, and mark it with a cross-stitch. Fig. 1 represents my cloth. I find the middle of the band, and mark it with a small line of basting stitches like Fig. 2. I make a line of running stitches for gathering. Now I draw these gathers into as small a space as possible, and wind the thread around a pin, and stroke my gathers; when this is done, I pin the ends of the gathered piece ⅛ in. from the ends of the band, like Fig. 3, and baste it to the band 1⁄16 in. below the gathering thread, fastening the ends securely by three over-sewing stitches down to the gathering thread, now holding the gathers toward me, take one back-stitch on every gather, take out the bastings, turn the band up from the gathers, baste and oversew the ends of the band; baste and hem the other edge of the band to the gathers, take one stitch in each gather. Fig. 4 shows band finished.

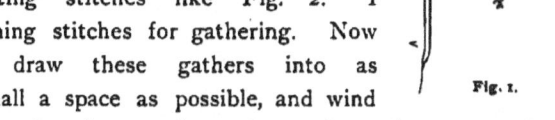

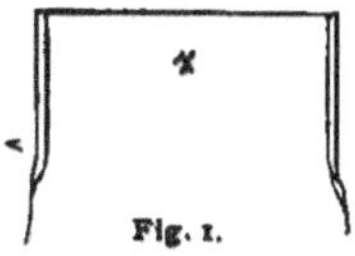

Fig. 1.

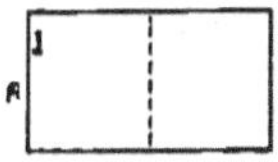

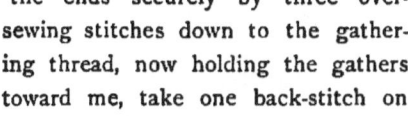

Fig. 2.

Fig. 3.

Fig. 4.

NELLIE E. JOHNSON

Heath School, Brookline, April 18, 1893.   (Age 14 years).

THE

ILLUSTRATIONS

in this book were made by the Half-tone and Photo-engraving processes of JOHN ANDREW & SON CO., whose methods are modern, practical, and economical. Estimates will be cheerfully given, at any time, upon illustrations for Textbooks, School Reports, Catalogues, etc. Write, for particulars and information, to

JOHN ANDREW & SON CO.,

ILLUSTRATORS,

196 Summer Street, Boston, Mass.

Prudent Purchasers save Time and Mental Friction

by careful discrimination in their selection of sewing materials. This group shows Silk, Button-Hole Twist, and Worsted Roll Braid, each bearing the name **Corticelli**, which is a guarantee of excellence. The reputation of this brand has been secured by fifty-two years of effort, attended by uninterrupted success. With this name on Silk, Twist, and Braid, — all of one shade, to match the garment and each other, — no thoughtful buyer hesitates.

NONOTUCK SILK CO., Sole Manufacturers.
Boston Salesroom, 18 Summer Street.

The only Improvement on the Tailors' Square ever Invented.

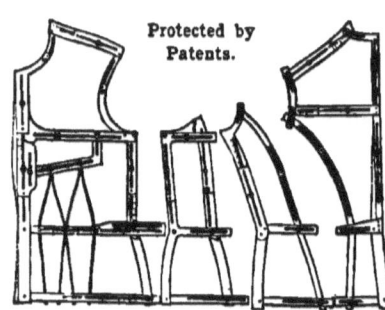

Protected by Patents.

The McDowell Garment Drafting Machine is now acknowledged to be the Standard System of Dressmaking throughout the world, as it is used in Edinburgh, Liverpool, London, Paris, and Berlin, and by all the best modistes and large establishments in this country.

Mrs. M. BAMFORTH, State Agent,
22 Winter Street, Boston, Mass.

MODEL FORMS

MANUFACTURED BY

S. N. UFFORD & SON, 12 West Street, Boston.

ONE SPECIALTY IS

LADIES' DRESS FORMS,

made one's EXACT SIZE and FIGURE,

CORRESPONDING TO THE PERSON.

WARRANTED.

On an exact model, not only can a lady make and fit her own dresses satisfactorily, but the form can be sent to the dressmaker, when the original may be hundreds of miles away, and never troubled with any tedious fitting and trying on.

www.ingramcontent.com/pod-product-compliance
Lightning Source LLC
Chambersburg PA
CBHW020105170426
43199CB00009B/395